A Dynamic Church: Spirit and Structure for the Seventies

W. L. HOWSE / W. O. THOMASON

A Dynamic Church

SPIRIT AND STRUCTURE FOR THE SEVENTIES

1970

Convention Press • Nashville, Tennessee

Requests for Church Study Course credit made prior to January 1, 1970, should be made in keeping with the requirements as set forth in the pamphlet "Trained Workmen." Credit for this book will be granted in category 1.

This book is number 6001
Library of Congress catalog card number: 79–75399
Printed in the United States of America
35.Jy69KSP

The Authors

W. L. Howse, DIRECTOR, EDUCATION DIVISION, the Sunday School Board of the Southern Baptist Convention, Nashville, Tennessee

W. O. Thomason, ASSISTANT TO THE DIRECTOR, Education Division, the Sunday School Board

George W. Schroeder, EXECUTIVE SECRETARY, Brotherhood Commission, Memphis, Tennessee, and commission staff

Howard B. Foshee, SECRETARY, CHURCH ADMINISTRATION DEPARTMENT, the Sunday School Board, and department staff

Wayne C. Todd, SECRETARY, CHURCH LIBRARY DEPARTMENT, the Sunday School Board, and department staff

W. Hines Sims, SECRETARY, CHURCH MUSIC DEPARTMENT, the Sunday School Board, and department staff

Bob M. Boyd, SECRETARY, CHURCH RECREATION DEPARTMENT, the Sunday School Board, and department staff

Philip B. Harris, SECRETARY, CHURCH TRAINING DEPARTMENT, the Sunday School Board, and department staff

A. V. Washburn, SECRETARY, SUNDAY SCHOOL DEPARTMENT, the Sunday School Board, and department staff

Alma Hunt, EXECUTIVE SECRETARY, Woman's Missionary Union, Birmingham, Alabama, and Promotion Division staff

Contents

The New Church Study Course

The New Church Study Course effective in January, 1970, is based on more than three years of study and design. It offers several improvements in the Church Study Course, which began in October, 1959. At that time three courses previously promoted by the Sunday School Board were merged: the Sunday School Training Course, the Graded Training Union Study Course, and the Church Music Training Course. Principles and methods books of the Woman's Missionary Union and the Brotherhood Commission were added in October, 1961 and January, 1967, respectively.

The New Church Study Course offers increased flexibility in meeting the needs of Southern Baptists. It provides courses of varying length and difficulty, varied formats and types of course materials, additional types of credit, and improved organization of courses.

The New Church Study Course consists of two series: the Christian Development Series for all church members, and the Christian Leadership Series for church leaders. Within each series, courses are organized into subject areas.

The purpose of the Christian Development Series is to provide courses of study which will help church members grow toward maturity in Christian living and competence in Christian service. The series offers more comprehensive, advanced, and varied learning experiences in subject areas of a church's educational program than can be provided through curriculum periodicals. It also provides tests and exercises, credits, and certificates of achievement which help church members measure their progress in developing needed knowledge, understanding, and skills. Units of instruction are provided for Preschoolers and Children. These are designed to reinforce foundational learnings. Materials which churches may use in recognizing the participation of Preschoolers and Children in these units are available from Baptist Book Stores.

The Christian Leadership Series provides a comprehensive series of courses organized into subject areas dealing with knowledge, understandings, and skills needed for effective church leadership. It provides tests and exercises, credits and diplomas to help leaders measure their growth in leadership ability. The Christian Leadership Series is the primary source for leadership training materials prepared by the agencies cooperating in the New Church Study Course.

Courses in both series are designed to be effective for individual and class study. Learning aids, study guides, and teaching guides are available for some courses. Credits are granted to Youth and Adults for reading, individual study, and class study.

The New Church Study Course is promoted by the Sunday School Board, 127 Ninth Avenue, North, Nashville, Tennessee 37203, through the departments in the Education Division; by the Woman's Missionary Union, 600 North Twentieth Street, Birmingham, Alabama 35203; by the Brotherhood Commission, 1548 Poplar Avenue, Memphis, Tennessee 38104; and by the respective departments in the state conventions affiliated with the Southern Baptist Convention.

A record of all credits, diplomas, and certificates earned should be maintained in each church.

Requirements for Credit

This book is the text for course 6001 of subject area Introductory Courses in Christian Leadership of the Christian Leadership Series, New Church Study Course. If credit is desired for this course through class study, individual study, or reading, the following requirements must be met:

I. Class work

    1. This course is designed for seven and one half (7½) hours of class study and carries three credits for such usage. If the course is studied in a class setting of less than seven and one half (7½) hours, the following criteria apply:

        (1) Five (5) class hours—two (2) credits

        (2) Two and one half (2½) class hours—one (1) credit

    The teacher will indicate the length of the class and the number of credits to be granted on the "Request for Course Credit" (Form 151).

    For courses in which laboratory experience or practice is desirable, two hours of such guided experience may be substituted as one hour of class time, provided at least half of the required hours are actually spent in class work.

2. A class member who attends all class sessions and completes the reading of the book as directed by the teacher will not be required to do any written work for credit.

3. A class member who is absent from one or more sessions must complete the required exercises or questions in the "Personal Learning Activities" section on all chapters he misses. In such a case, he must turn in his paper by the date the teacher sets (usually within ten days following the last class). Also, he must certify that he has read the book.

4. The teacher should request an award for himself. A person who teaches a course for Youth or Adults (in any subject area) will be granted the same number of credits as class members. The teacher of an approved unit of study for Preschoolers and Children will be granted two credits in course 2299 in subject area 22 of the Christian Leadership Series. Request award by using Form 151.

5. The director of QUEST or the teacher of the course should complete the "Request for Course Credit" (Form 151) and forward it after completion of the class to the Church Study Course Awards Office, 127 Ninth Avenue, North, Nashville, Tennessee 37203.

II. Individual Study

1. A person who wishes to complete this course without attending class sessions may receive full credit by certifying that he has read the book and by completing all exercises or questions in the "Personal Learning Activities" section.

2. Students may find profit in studying the text together, but individual papers are required. Carbon copies or duplicates of the answers cannot be accepted.

3. The work required for individual study credit should be turned in for checking to the director of QUEST or the person designated by the church to administer the Christian Leadership Series. The form entitled "Request for Course Credit" (Form 151) must be used in requesting these awards. It is to be forwarded by the director of QUEST or the person designated by the Church Study

Course Awards Office, 127 Ninth Avenue, North, Nashville, Tennessee 37203.

III. Reading Credit

1. A person may receive one credit toward the diploma on which he is working by reading this book.
2. Upon completion of the reading, he must complete the "Request for Course Credit" (Form 151). He should give the completed form to the director of QUEST or to the person designated by his church to be responsible for administering the Christian Leadership Series.
3. The director of QUEST or the person designated by the church will see that the request is completed, signed, and forwarded to the Church Study Course Awards Office, 127 Ninth Avenue, North, Nashville, Tennessee 37203.

IV. Awards and Records

Two copies of the course credit award form will be sent by the Church Study Course Awards Office to the church. One copy should be filed in the church-training record and the other given to the individual.

Preface

A Dynamic Church is the successor to *A Church Organized and Functioning*. It is not, however, an old book with a new name.

The concepts and terminology expressed in the first edition (1963) of *A Church Organized and Functioning* were approved by a limited number of church and denominational program leaders. Consequently, each copy of the first edition included a questionnaire for evaluation and feedback.

Hundreds of questionnaires were returned, most of which supported the concepts of the nature, purpose, functions, tasks, and programs of a church as expressed in the book. Information from the questionnaires contributed to improving the 1966 edition of *A Church Organized and Functioning*.

In 1965 the Southern Baptist Convention launched comprehensive plans for obtaining its emphasis for the seventies. The Convention's church program and service leaders felt they could make a greater contribution to the success of the emphasis if they could establish a base upon which to plan program suggestions and materials for the churches. The concepts expressed in *A Church Organized and Functioning* offered the best beginning point in stating this base.

The Church Program and Services Subcommittee of the Inter-Agency Council's Coordinating Committee engaged in a study of the task and program statements and made appropriate revisions. These statements were shared with church and denominational program leaders for refinement. Both the Coordinating Committee and the Inter-Agency Council approved the revised draft.

When the Southern Baptist Convention approved 1969–73 as Phase I of the 70 Onward Emphasis, the Inter-Agency Council voted to use the revised statements of church tasks and programs as the church program base for offering assistance to churches during this period. *A Dynamic Church* expresses these statements in terms of the church's nature, life, and work in the seventies' setting.

The process which led to the production of this new manuscript makes it more than a book. It is a basic document which unites denominational leadership in support of the churches as they seek to fulfil their mission and purpose. It already has gone a long way toward unifying, correlating, and coordinating denominational assistance for the churches.

A Dynamic Church is also a basic instrument which churches may use in understanding themselves and how they can expect to be assisted in becoming more truly the people of God.

The book will not be revised until 1973. The revision will become the base for programing for Phase II of the Southern Baptist Convention's emphasis covering the years 1973–79.

Churches which invest sufficient time to get a working knowledge of the content of this book will be able to make the fullest possible use of the new things which will be offered them during the seventies. The book should be studied by every church leader and member immediately. Classes in its study should be offered periodically through 1973. Church leaders should keep a copy handy and read it often for new insights and meaning.

The concepts expressed will not be grasped in quick reading or in a study during a few nights. Those who have dealt with these ideas since 1961 gain new understanding of them through continued use.

We who wrote the manuscript are committed to establishing and strengthening churches according to the teachings of the New Testament. Our earnest prayer is that what is offered here will contribute to reaching this objective.

1. The Church: Meant for Humanity

What is a church? What did God establish his churches to do? What does he continue to establish his churches to do? Are churches theocracies? Democracies? Both?

Perhaps the best word to define a Southern Baptist church is found in a combination of the two words "theocracy" and "democracy." Webster's new dictionary uses the term "theodemocracy" to define a community governed by people according to the revealed will of the deity. A theodemocracy calls for such democratic processes as discussion and decision-making to discover what the body should do under God's leadership and direction.

To understand this unique and different body requires a study of the biblical basis of the nature, purpose, and functions of a church.

THE BIBLICAL BASIS OF A CHURCH

The Bible teaches that God created man a free spiritual being in direct relationship with himself. Man at the beginning was in partnership and fellowship with God. Man was a reflection of God's unity. "And God said, Let us make man in our image, after our likeness. . . . So God created man in his own image" (Gen. 1:26–27).

This partnership of man with God was broken by man's dis-

1

obedience. The power of sin came between man and God and between man and man. However, the world still belonged to God, and God had a continuing desire to restore fellowship and partnership with man.

The story of redemption which began in the garden reveals God's continuing love for humanity and his desire to reveal himself more perfectly to man. One revelation of God and his purpose for man came as he created a unique community through a series of divine covenantal acts (Ex. 19:4–6, 29:45–46; Isa. 43:1–7, 49:1–12; Amos 3:1–2; Mic. 6:4). This partnership or covenant of God with the Jewish people did not begin with the people but with him. It was God who called the community or congregation of people into being. But such a congregation could be accomplished only through obedience to his will. It was God who called Abraham and made him the father of his people. It was God who summoned Moses to rescue a slave nation and forge it into a religious community through the law at Sinai. And it was God who over and over again called his covenant community back to its true nature through the prophets. The whole sweep of the Old Testament is the thrilling story of God's creation of a "holy people," a kingdom of priests, a new kind of human community.

It is to be noted that these were God's people only if in their community life they were obedient to the divine law of the covenant. The prophets belittled the external ceremonies and rites and called the people to moral obedience. "What doth the Lord require of thee, but to do justly, and to love mercy, and to walk humbly with thy God?" (Mic. 6:8). According to the prophets, God was constructing a community along the lines of justice and mercy—a community in which the poor were neither robbed nor oppressed, and the widow and the fatherless were cared for and protected.

God's purpose then in forming this community was to create a new kind of people, among whom mercy replaced vindictiveness and justice replaced oppression.

In the New Testament, the church is a continuation of God's plan, but it is even more than a covenant people. The New Testment concept of God's called-out people was a new beginning for the whole human race. The new covenant was not a divine law addressed to a particular people. It was the crucified and risen Lord who had brought all men into right relationship with God. The church became the new humanity in Christ: "For as in Adam all die, even so in Christ shall all be made alive" (1 Cor. 15:22).

"The church, in its inclusive sense, is the fellowship of persons redeemed by Christ and made one in the family of God." [1] The church is composed of all redeemed persons of all time.

The church in every age finds expression in churches. Churches are established by Christ to do his work in the world. A particular church may live and die, but his church moves on triumphantly.

A Dynamic Church has been written to help every church see itself in terms of what Christ established it to do. Church members must understand the organism of which they are a part. They must see and feel themselves as functioning members of a body in fellowship with Christ and with one another. Such understandings and relationships can come only as church members understand the mission and work of New Testament churches.

The New Testament church was a congregation, a fellowship of redeemed people, a spiritual community. It was neither a building nor a hierarchy. It was an ecclesia, a gathering of people called out by God into a new kind of community. Christ was its head, and although it had men as leaders, its true life and leadership was from above.

Paul could write to the Corinthian Christians that they were "the church of God," because they were "sanctified in Christ Jesus" and called "upon the name of Jesus Christ our Lord" (1 Cor. 1:2). Again, Paul referred to the Christians at Ephesus as "the church of God, which he hath purchased with his own blood" (Acts 20:28). It is clear that the churches were brought into being by Jesus, and that he did it by his death—which to Paul included the resurrection as the climax of his death.

Paul said very clearly: "Therefore if any man be in Christ, he is a new creature: old things are passed away; behold, all

---

[1] "Baptist Ideals," a tract published by the Sunday School Board of the Southern Baptist Convention, Nashville, Tennessee, 1963, p. 8.

things are become new" (2 Cor. 5:17). The emphasis is on the word "new." What is this newness of life? Paul wrote that God gave his new people the ministry of reconciliation. He also wrote that Christians are ambassadors for Christ, partners and co-workers, even to the extent of appearing in Christ's stead (2 Cor. 5:20).

Churches today stand in their finest hour. Members must dare to believe that Jesus is lord and that day-by-day events are in his rule. God's redemptive purpose will be achieved in spite of the ruthlessness of sinful men. When men and nations are being plunged into hopelessness and despair by war, greed, and the quest for power, the church must counteract with a bold faith.

In their early beginning, church members were confronted with persecution, poverty, political intimidation, military might, imprisonment, and even death. Yet the small band of God's redeemed, without money, power, political influence, or military might, held firm in their faith even to death.

THE NATURE OF A CHURCH

Apart from Jesus Christ there could be no churches. Churches owe their existence to God. The life and vitality of the early church was made evident by the coming of the Holy Spirit at Pentecost. A church finds its meaning and dynamic through Jesus Christ and the Holy Spirit. The Scriptures reveal the nature of a church.

A church comes into being because people experience new life in Christ. The unity of people who are "born from above" makes a church. A church is dependent on the redemption of individuals through their acceptance of Jesus Christ as Saviour and Lord.

The kinship of Christians with one another is more than friendship. It is described as "fellowship." "That which we have seen and heard," wrote John, "declare we unto you, that ye also may have fellowship with us: and truly our fellowship is with the Father, and with his Son Jesus Christ" (1 John 1:3). To belong to Christ is to have the nature to belong to all other Christians. The Greek word "koinonia," which is translated fellowship, is used to describe the bond that unites Christians. In Christ Christians find they have many differences but no true spiritual distinctions. A church is a unique relationship of people who come together and remain together because they accept and follow the lordship of Christ.

The basic element in this fellowship is love. It is the kind of love expressed by God who gave his son for man's salvation. "Herein is love, not that we loved God, but that he loved us, and sent his Son to be the propitiation for our sins. Beloved, if God so loved us, we ought also to love one another" (1 John 4:10-11).

This love for one another was the crowning test of fellowship. It went beyond the church fellowship, and expressed itself for all mankind. "There is neither Jew nor Greek, there is neither bond nor free, there is neither male nor female: for ye are all one in Christ Jesus" (Gal. 3:28).

Augustine wrote: "The true Christian will never set himself up over other men. . . . If you would be better than another man, you will grudge to see him as your equal. You ought to wish all men equal to yourself; and if you have gone beyond another man in wisdom, you should want him to show himself wise. . . . See how he (Paul) wanted all to be his equals; and just because charity made him so desire, he was raised above all. Man has transgressed his proper limit: . . . he has let covetousness carry him away, so that he might be higher than other men. And that is pride." [2]

Fellowship is developed further through the New Testament concept of believers as the household or family of God. Jesus said that all who believed in him were his family. They were his brothers, his sisters, his mother (Mark 3:33-35). To be identified with Christ is to be identified with all whom Christ loves. Christian fellowship is the only means to overcome the barriers which men have erected against one another.

Stephen defended himself before his accusers, insisting that God's concern for men could not be limited to the Jews alone (Acts 7). Soon Philip took the gospel to the Samaritans (Acts 8:4-25). Later Simon Peter went to the home of Cornelius and

---

[2] John Burnaby (trans.), *Augustine: Later Works* ("The Library of Christian Classics," Vol. VIII, London: SCM Press, 1955), pp. 321-22.

declared that God had poured out his spirit upon the Gentiles (Acts 10:45).

The fellowship of God's people is such that "it crosses all barriers of age, social status, nation, race, and interest, creating one body in Christ, a fellowship of . . . 'equally condemned and equally forgiven sinners.' " [3]

Thus far a church has been discussed as the new humanity, the people of God, bound together in a fellowship, fulfilling God's plan. A church is more than this. It is also the body of Christ in which the living Spirit of the risen Lord dwells. Paul wrote to the church in Corinth: "Now ye are the body of Christ, and members in particular" (1 Cor. 12:27).

A church is not formed by mutual agreement to come together at a certain time on a certain day. It is formed fundamentally by God's calling each believer through his word, and by his presence in grace and power in the midst of his faithful congregation. A church is more than the individuals who make it up. The "more" is the presence of the risen Lord in the congregation, communicating himself in his word, and having fellowship with members of the congregation.

This concept can be more clearly developed in comparing the purpose of the Jewish Temple and that of a church. The Temple was dedicated as a place where God chose to dwell in the midst of his people. It was the place of worship, the place where the priests made sacrifice for sin. People came to the Temple to learn the law, to dedicate their children, and to seek God's presence. But the Temple failed to achieve its purposes. Men desecrated, defiled, and destroyed it. Jesus indicted those responsible for the Temple for not fulfilling its purpose (Matt. 21:12–13).

The old Temple was replaced by the body of Christ. From henceforth God would meet man in Christ. When asked for a sign of his authority Christ said: "Destroy this temple, and in three days I will raise it up" (John 2:19). The temple Christ referred to was his physical body. If Christ's body was the true

---

[3] Donald G. Miller, *The Nature and Mission of the Church* (Richmond: John Knox Press, 1957), p. 30.

temple, how has it continued to serve as the temple? The
answer is found at Pentecost. After Jesus had died, risen, and
ascended to the right hand of God, he returned in his spirit to
live in his churches. Churches now carry on the purpose of
the temple, but in a vastly different way. By virtue of Christ's
presence, each church becomes the body of Christ of which
members are living (physical) stones. Knowing and feeling this
relationship to Christ should give new life and effort to every
church member.

THE FUNCTIONS OF A CHURCH

Paul declared the church to be the body of Christ, with
Christ as its head. This means that a church looks to Christ to
establish its work. This work may be thought of as its functions. A church function then is an essential action without
which its basic nature would be altered. In seeking to clarify
the work of churches for the seventies, the chairmen of forty-one
special study groups in 1965 named and defined five functions of
a church. They are worship, witness, education, ministry, and
application. These functions are not independent of each other,
nor are they done in sequence. They are interdependent and
interrelated.

1. Worship

Worship is a personal encounter with God in which the
Christian experiences a deepening of his faith and a strengthening of his service. Worship is central to the Christian life. It is
relationship to God, a conscious entrance into his presence. It
is the most direct touch that people have with God. Worship
is a response to the presence of God.

God is in the midst of his people, and through worship
there is a response to his presence in adoration and praise, in
confession of sin and repentance, and in thanksgiving and service. The objective of worship is to exalt the presence of God.

The particular form, symbols, or media of worship depend
on each church. The forms of worship may vary and change,
but when one responds affirmatively to the presence of God,
worship is taking place.

Worship is never consummated until the worshiper serves.
The response to God's presence indicates the reality of the experience.

2. Witness

Witness is the proclaiming of God's work of grace in Christ
for all men. New Testament churches are characterized by
their proclamation that Jesus Christ is alive and the Saviour
of the world. Early believers were so bold in their witnessing
that they were imprisoned, tortured, persecuted, and martyred.

A church must lead its members to witness with power to
their own encounter with Christ. A living faith in Christ must
speak out. Any retreat, withdrawal, or silence on the lordship
of Christ destroys the influence of Christians and the life of a
church. A church succeeds only by sharing the good news
of redemption.

The decade of the 70's will require new methods in witnessing. It is apparent that a church must go to the people and
tell the good news before the people will come and hear. Personal witnessing about Jesus Christ is the day-to-day means by
which a church fulfils its true purpose. Jesus said: "Ye shall
be witnesses unto me" (Acts 1:8) .

3. Education

To educate is to guide persons in their progressive development toward Christian maturity. This includes leading, teaching,
training, and involving persons in growing toward a mature
Christian faith and life.

Learning was a necessity for the life of the early churches.
Members knew that converts coming from a pagan world had
to learn basic Christian beliefs. Jesus had commanded them to
teach all nations. The Christian life was to be a continuous
learning experience. Christians were to continue to teach what
Christ had taught them.

Unless a church teaches its members, they will become ignorant
of the beliefs and doctrines as well as the ethical standards of
Christianity. Education is essential for church members. Christ
rules his churches as members hear the Word proclaimed and

taught. Thus, preaching and teaching are primary means through which the Word becomes alive in a church.

Christian growth is dependent on learning, just as physical growth is dependent on eating. A church that fails to educate its members hinders not only their growth but its own growth as a church.

4. Ministry

When a church meets crucial human needs in the spirit of Christ, it is performing the function of ministry. "Minister" and "serve" come from the same root word. Each Christian is a servant or minister. A pastor is a servant of servants. When he "ad-ministers" a church, he is multiplying his ministry by serving through others. This concept of one of the roles of a pastor is as basic as the concept of his role in proclamation. Jesus knew what was in man and always placed himself in a servant role. Even when performing miracles he was a servant. The tone of Jesus' life was set in the words: "The Son of Man came not to be ministered unto, but to minister, and to give his life a ransom for many" (Matt. 20:28). Persons in need cried out to Jesus. He never let these cries go unheeded.

The church exists for people—those who are members of the body as well as those who live without the Saviour. Where human need exists, the church has a responsibility to minister. Paul exhorted the Christians: "We then that are strong ought to bear the infirmities of the weak, and not to please ourselves" (Rom. 15:1).

5. Application

To apply means the practical application of Christian principles in all the issues of everyday life. Christianity is both word and deed, belief and behavior, faith and practice. It is possible to know the Bible and not apply it. All that God reveals through his Word is for application to life. Every conflict between right and wrong demands the application of Christian principles.

This function of a church accents the need for Christians to seek the mind of Christ in the issues of life. Each person is free in Christ, but not free to his own interpretation of what is right and wrong. The guiding truth for every Christian is to discover the mind of Christ on each issue or problem and apply that truth with courage.

Such an application determines one's vote for public officials, one's conduct of business, one's relationship to his family, and one's standards of public and private morality. James wrote: "Be ye doers of the word, and not hearers only" (James 1:22).

2. The Church: Its Response to Changing Conditions

Churches are central in God's plan for world redemption. The place of each church is never more prominent than in a disordered and changing society. God's purpose for churches has not changed. Conditions under which churches must work are changing. Churches must be sensitive to these conditions and adjust their methods and approaches accordingly. A church should not change just to be different.

THE CERTAINTY OF CHANGE

It is incorrect to say that everything changes or that there are no limits to change. Man's nature is evil: that fact does not change. Man envies and hates, and schemes: that fact does not change. Man dies: that fact does not change.

Other things, however, do change year by year. Man travels faster, eats better food, lives in more comfort, knows more about his world, and has more knowledge than his ancestors. While some men enjoy these benefits, others live in the communities where they were born, eat less, and know little more than their grandfathers.

Change generally alters the less important, the form and circumstances, the setting and surroundings, and the instrument and conditions of life. Seldom does change alter the essence of life—those fundamental things that bring sorrow and joy to humanity.

This is why a church cannot continue doing its work as usual. A church must discover people as they are and seek to lead them into God's fellowship. God is at work in his churches and through them in the world. God is also personally at work in the world. The destiny of the world is in his will. Churches must discover what God wants them to do with him in the world. They must be obedient to getting his work accomplished. A church is a responding community, a people whose task is to discern the presence of God in the world and to join in his work.

THE STRUGGLE WITH STRUCTURE

When conditions change radically, a church is usually forced to identify its basic message and method of work. The message must not change, but a church must find new methods to reach people with the gospel. If a church wants to reach Sunday workers, should it offer Bible study at another time during the week?

When both parents work, should churches establish day care centers, kindergartens, and after school classes to assure parents and children of adequate care? Many churches that are doing this are filling previously empty buildings five days a week with persons who one day will meet the Master of this ministry.

How should a church relate its message to poverty and wealth? Southern Baptist churches are wrestling with this problem even now. A church can provide fellowship for the poor, the wealthy, and those between these extremes. Persons of all conditions and circumstances in life can be made to feel at home in the same church if the spirit of Christ prevails. While churches attract members according to their location, they should not become "typed" as to the members they have. All members are equal in God's sight. Any man in need of the gospel and a church fellowship should find both in any Baptist church he enters.

One of the chief obstacles in the path of Jesus was the loyalty of religious leaders to tradition. Jesus confronted controversy in allowing his disciples to eat without having previously washed their hands (Matt. 15:20). Much of what Jesus said in his Sermon on the Mount was in contradiction to the understanding passed along through the religious tradition. Jesus said: "Ye have heard that it was said of them of old time . . . but I say unto you." The Pharisees and Sadducees, religious leaders of the day, could not accept Jesus because of their devotion to the past and to the tradition of the elders.

Eric Hoffer in *The Ordeal of Change* draws a descriptive picture of the conflict in Jesus' day between the intellectuals and the masses. "The noble carpenter from Galilee could make no headway when he challenged the pretension of the solemn scholars, hair-splitting lawyers, and arrogant pedants, and raised his voice in defense of the poor in spirit. He was ostracized and anathematized, and his teachings found a following chiefly among non-Jews.[1]

Jesus was a radical to the people of his day. He was a threat to the power of political leaders. He was a blasphemer and distorter of truth to the religious leaders. Yet Jesus, in reality, was a light shining in the darkness. He said that he did not come to destroy the law and the prophets but to fulfil them. People's understanding of God could be compared with a half-filled glass of water. Jesus did not come to pour out the water but to pour in more that the glass might be filled.

A church must be true to its basic nature, purpose, and functions. But it must express these in terms every generation can understand. Churches have a divine reason for being. This includes the injunction: "Be not conformed to this world: but be ye transformed by the renewing of your mind" (Rom. 12:2). Churches are not bound to tradition, but to the living word.

The book of Acts is exciting reading because first-century Christians proclaimed the gospel with power to their pagan generation. They were empowered by the Spirit to challenge religious tradition and the sins of their generation. Acts begins with the noise of a rushing, mighty wind empowering the church, and closes with a giant storm shipwrecking a missionary. Just as God sent his Son into the world, the Lord has

---

[1] Eric Hoffer, *The Ordeal of Change* (New York: Harper & Row Publishers, 1963), pp. 40–41.

always sent his people into the world. Whenever God's people become active in his world, conflict and controversy result. But controversy often produces change just as change produces controversy. Mark (chapter 1) gives an account of Jesus' commanding the unclean spirits to come out of a man. The evil spirits, having torn him, came out. There was convulsion and then expulsion—controversy within and then change. In this sense, controversy is an instrument of victory.

The uproar at Ephesus (Acts 19) was a controversy between the traditional worshipers of the goddess Diana and the preachers of the new gospel of Jesus Christ. In the end, God's will prevailed, and a church was established at Ephesus.

THE RESPONSIBILITY FOR RELEVANCY

Today's church cannot escape the responsibility for making the gospel relevant to persons in their human situation. To do so one must know people as they are. What is it like to be a youth, an eccentric, a deviate, a middle of the roader, or a social outcast? Relevancy means to communicate in language the unchurched can understand. Can a church excuse itself from any arena of human life?

Jesus was concerned about all men and all of each man: his body, mind, spirit, environment, future, ideas, relationships, burdens, sins, handicaps, struggles, and sufferings. Whatever concerned man concerned Jesus. The Lord first sought to lead a man to God and then to lead him in paths of righteousness. This was not always possible. Yet Christ never rejected a man because he continued in unbelief.

When Jesus fed more than five thousand people fish and bread, he revealed his personal concern for their hunger. After the multitude had eaten, Jesus told them his discipleship required total commitment. The crowd murmured that this was a hard saying. They turned away. Why did Jesus bother to feed the crowd? Would it not have been easier to preach and let them go? Was not Jesus' concern for the total needs of the people?

Oliver Cromwell described the results of irrelevance when he said: "A man never goes so far as when he does not know whither he is going." This can also be said of a church. Recently a church building was up for sale. The congregation of twelve members offered the building for a price under $75,000. Any conservative estimate would have priced the beautiful structure, with its appointments, for three times that price. The church building was within five miles of a million people. Why was a building surrounded by such a host of people for sale? The answer was simple: the church had ceased to have a relevant mission to its community. In the building was a battery of ovens for baking bread, a large gymnasium, carpeted floors, and beautiful wooden pews. The church had turned its eyes inward. Its primary purpose had become the care for itself. So the people of the community got bread from stores, played in the streets, and ignored the message and activity of the people in the big stone church. The church and the lost people had missed each other.

Americans place great value on political power, wealth, social status, and educational and professional attainment. A successful man in one of these areas is often acceptable for leadership in a church regardless of his spiritual attainment. This is because status symbols of a society are easily transferred to the churches within it. These attainments are symbols of influence, but a church cannot substitute secular symbols for spiritual values.

If the church is God's plan for redeeming lost men, then it must speak to men as they are and where they are, regardless of who they are. A church must know not only who it is but also what it must be doing. The church has both a message and a mission in the world. The mind that thinks of Negroes, Indians, and Mexicans as slaves and servants will have difficulty in accepting these people as heirs of God and joint heirs with Christ.

The next decade will bring population changes that the churches of Jesus Christ have never faced in 2,000 years of existence. By 1975 there will be about 64 million people under fifteen years of age. Not quite 50 million will be between fifteen and twenty-five years of age. How will the church prevail in a preponderantly youthful society?

Can the church meet the challenge of a three- or four-day weekend? Does extended leisure time mean that a church must extend its witness to mountain and seashore?

Consider the critical problems of people in large urban areas.

Crime, poverty, slum areas, delinquency, race relations, recreation, politics, and education will challenge the churches in fulfilling their God-given purpose.

These changes will not frustrate God or change his purpose for the church. The assurance that the Lord is still with his people is as strong today as when Paul escaped Damascus hidden in a basket.

When Jesus told his disciples, "I will build my church; and the gates of hell shall not prevail against it" (Matt. 16:18) he spoke aggressively, not passively. It is not a question of waiting for satanic powers to hurl themselves against the church. It is the church pressing the battle to the very gates of evil. It is storming the citadel to bring release and redemption from sin. When the churches challenge, the gates will fall.

THE FREEDOM TO RESPOND

A study of New Testament churches reveals that each church was the only one of its kind. When John wrote in Revelation of the seven churches, he described characteristics of each. The church at Ephesus was characterized by a fading love for Christ; the church at Smyrna was suffering persecution; the church at Pergamos fought paganism; the church at Thyatira needed to purge its membership; the church at Sardis performed imperfect works; the church at Philadelphia was strong in its faith; and the church at Laodicea was without conviction for good or evil (Rev. 2–3).

Two of the most important churches described in the book of Acts were at Jerusalem and Antioch. The Jerusalem church was motherly, stately, and doctrinally strong. The church at Antioch was warmhearted and full of missionary zeal.

Churches were different because they ministered in different parts of the world. The variety in ministry demonstrated both freedom in, and devotion to, Christ. It is Christ who gives freedom. Because the church is under his lordship, there is a dependency on him for direction and guidance.

Each body of believers must confront the world with its own resources and methods. Just as Jesus ministered differently to people so churches must minister through different methods and forms. Many things may hinder churches in exercising such freedom. Often, however, it is the lack of concern to be effective in ministry. Sometimes it is the fear of failure in a new undertaking. The spirit of Christ calls churches to seek victories. Victories in a changing world like the seventies demand creativity and boldness. The church in the upper room was transformed on the day of Pentecost by the presence of the Spirit. The church moved freely from behind the closed doors to the streets of Jerusalem. Depressed and anxious disciples became bold witnesses, speaking in unknown but understandable languages. The experience was opposite to that of Babel. At the tower of Babel God confused men's tongues, and they spoke confusion. At Pentecost God freed their tongues. Peter said: "Let me freely speak unto you" (Acts 2:29).

The greatest problem a church faces is that of converting its faith to action. Faith in Christ gives courage to break the chains of fear and defeat. It challenges the impossible. When Jesus brought Lazarus from the dead, he said, "Loose him, and let him go" (John 11:44). By analogy, every member of a church is a Lazarus with new life and power through Christ. And every church is Christ alive in the world. The Church is free and empowered to act. Such freedom is characterized by flexibility and freshness. Such power is characterized by wisdom and love. A church should approach every situation, realizing that its final judge will be Christ. The paradox is that the judge is also a witness.

The charismatic gifts of the Holy Spirit are varied. Not all people possess the same kind of quality of gifts. Yet all are used for God's glory. So the church made up of spirit-filled people is empowered to overcome regardless of circumstances. A church must "walk by faith, not by sight" (2 Cor. 5:7).

3. The Church: Structured for the Seventies

Historians are slow to evaluate history because events are tied together with elastic bands. Events that occur in one year may influence life for hundreds of years. Even though the Protestant Reformation occurred over four hundred years ago, the results continue to influence thinking today.

From all perspectives, the 1970's will be a decade of destiny for Southern Baptists. The Inter-Agency Council of the Southern Baptist Convention has made studies to find out what churches are now doing and what they are thinking for the years ahead. From these studies came new insights which challenge churches to evaluate their mission. To emphasize the opportunities ahead the Convention has planned for the next decade under the compelling idea of "70 Onward."

DECADE OF DESTINY

Most people agree that the church is facing a transformation. This transformation is what some have called renewal. All predictions indicate that the seventies will be a period of rapid change for churches as well as society. When life is stable, most activity becomes routine and repetitious. When society is in reformation or revolution, many problems do not repeat themselves. The frontier of a changing society is where the people are. The church should not be at the rear of man's search for a better life. It should lead the way.

George MacLeod, founder of the Iona Community, writes: "Jesus was not crucified in a cathedral between two candles, but on a cross between two thieves; on the town garbage-heap; at a crossroads so cosmopolitan that they had to write his title in Hebrew and in Latin and in Greek . . . ; at the kind of place where cynics talk smut, and thieves curse, and soldiers gamble. Because that is where He died. . . . That is where churchmen should be and what churchmanship should be about." [1]

Some challenges appear immediately ahead for churches. We will not be permitted much time to structure ourselves to respond. One can sense as he reads that many of the following will need a major response by the mid-seventies or not at all. To respond to these challenges a church must not neglect its proclamation of the gospel and its other essential activities. Rather, it will see in these challenges new ways for the gospel to be applied to life as it is being lived.

Churches must consider the condition of family life and develop a Christian view for contemporary family living. The church cannot replace the family any more than families can replace the church. Parents have responsibilities for children that are God given. These cannot be delegated to the church. While struggling for its own survival, a church must not take away the life of a family. There is a need for a joint effort of the church and the home in the education of children and youth. Emphasis is needed on the sacredness of marriage and the obligations of parents and children to each other.

Churches should reflect a greater community awareness. Churches can be an integral part of all the community's life. There is a relationship between the church on the corner, the bank across the street, and the gasoline service station on the opposite corner. These institutions do not exist in isolation. Jesus made honest tax collectors out of Matthew and Zacchaeus. The woman at the well was confronted at the town's public water supply. Whose water was in the well? Whose energy is supplied by the service station?

---

[1] George Fielder MacLeod, *Only One Way Left* (Glasgow: Iona Community, 1956), p. 38.

The church has a burden for the honesty and happiness of bank employees, service station attendants, garbage collectors, cooks, farmers, and executives. There is no way to avoid a responsibility to everybody that touches the people in the community. Where there is pain, sorrow, and suffering, the church must offer healing. Where there is fraud, injustice, and evil, the church must offer grace. Where there is depression and discouragement, the church must offer hope and faith. Where there is hate, envy, and disorder, the church must exercise and teach love and understanding. A church must be in the community as leaven is in the bread.

Churches must combat the depersonalizing elements in the community. People tend to become classified as the "postman," "the insurance agent," and "the service man." As far as identification by name, family, hopes, and ambitions are concerned, these people could be robots. This is one of the characteristics Harvey Cox writes about in *The Secular City:*

> A recent survey by some Protestant ministers in a new urban highrise apartment area illustrates the misplaced emphases on the I-thou (person-church) relationships. . . . In conducting their study, the pastors were shocked to discover that the recently arrived apartment dwellers, whom they expected to be lonely and desperate for relationships, did not want to meet their neighbors socially and had no interest whatever in church or community groups. At first the ministers deplored what they called a "social pathology" and a "hedgehog psychology." Later, however, they found that what they had encountered was a sheer survival technique.[2]

Soon in rural areas people will be replaced with automatic machinery. Predictions indicate that in the seventies farming will be done with computers. A control panel will beam its signals from steel towers to operate tractors, irrigation, electric feeders, and even the collection of eggs. The absent farm owner who lives in a city several hundred miles away will have little interest in the church. The rural or pastoral life may soon be gone. Rural churches must prepare for such a possibility. This does not mean the rural church has no place. These churches must restudy their ministry within such a community.

---

[2] Harvey Cox, *The Secular City* (New York: Macmillan Co., 1965), p. 44.

Churches must also decide how they will relate to the services and resources within the community. There are many governmental agencies doing social work and attempting to relieve human needs. What about labor unions? What about the poor? Baptist churches must not forget the common man with his aspirations and desires. Our affluent society will continue to spawn the poor and underprivileged. Church may capitulate to one type of culture only to emerge with a conformity that kills the spirit. Baptists must remember their beginnings and their history. Churches must see that their mission is to all humanity.

Churches must consider their relationship to other churches. If two or more churches acknowledge Christ as Lord (Rom. 10:9–10), there is a kinship. Kinship does not require identical life styles. Neither should it require isolation and enmity. Two department stores may exist side-by-side with a common interest in the city and its welfare. They may meet jointly to consider mutual business problems. Nevertheless, the stores feel that they offer a desirable distinctive service to the community. In the same way, churches should have Christian relationships without destroying one another. This was the fundamental meaning in our constitutional guarantee of religious freedom. Downtown churches, suburban churches, new missions, and churches with strength should not seek to weaken and undermine one another, but rather to complement one another in fulfilling their objective.

Churches should seek to understand the demands and requirements for their pastors in the years ahead. Every effort should be made by churches to develop clear relationships between the pastors and church members. As the body of Christ, the church does not belong to the pastor or the members. There is an increasing need for members to participate and to lead. Pastors must fulfil their role as God's prophets. Congregations should insist that they do so and support them in this role. They must share the leadership role with competent unordained members without fear of being outdone.

STRUCTURE FOR THE SEVENTIES

A variety of special ministries as well as variety in established ministries will be needed to respond to the challenges of the seventies. A church may require new or enlarged programs to meet the needs of the church constituency, the people of the community, and groups across the nation or around the world.

Our specialized world with its advances in science and technology is creating many subgroups with special needs. Add these to those already a part of our history and the result is a task beyond the capacity of a single church. The seventies may be the decade when one Baptist church will offer a ministry that others in the community do not. Whatever the case, when needs arise that a church can meet, there must be a way to respond. Churches must be prepared to utilize the best methods, equipment, and techniques. Leaders should be trained in skills to meet demands.

1. Stating a Church Objective

In light of the challenges and variety of possibilities presented, a church should review and evaluate its objective. Do the Scriptures or the church's constitution call for a more limited mission than that described? Is the mission described broad enough? The Great Commission has served most often as the stated objective of churches. In seeking to relate this commission to the 1970's, the Southern Baptist Convention included the following objective in the '70 Onward Emphasis. It was primarily for use as guidance to Convention agencies, but it may be of equal value to churches preparing for the decade ahead.

"The objective of a church, composed of baptized believers who share a personal commitment to Jesus Christ as Savior and Lord, is to be a redemptive body in Christ, through the power of the Holy Spirit, growing toward Christian maturity through worship, witness, education, and ministry, proclaiming the gospel to the whole world, and applying Christian principles to man and society that God's purposes may be achieved." [3]

A church, if it is to fulfil its nature, cannot neglect its objective. The objective should be sought not only by individual

---

[3] "The '70 Onward Report to the Southern Baptist Convention, Miami Beach," a progress report by '70 Onward Study Groups presented to, and adopted by, the Southern Baptist Convention meeting in Miami Beach, Florida, May 30–June 2, 1967, pp. 3–4.

members but also through the actions of the body working as a whole and in subgroups. Every person in the church should feel the necessity of sharing in the achievement of the objective. An objective is simply the statement of a church's intentions. Intentions are a church's aspirations stated in terms that combine biblical commands and human needs. Intentions convey the hopes and aspirations for the church's future. They challenge persons and organizations to strive, to innovate, to risk, and to make commitments. Intentions may be greatly influenced by the past, but they are always expressed in terms of the future.

2. Identifying Church Tasks

Seldom can a church start from a state of unpreparedness and make a quick impact in meeting major needs of its constituency or community. Effective ministry can be launched best from an established base. The identification of tasks and programs provides this base of operation. Churches are urged to establish their base carefully in order that they may have a maximum of mobility, flexibility, and strength for mission.

Tasks are defined as basic continuing activities of primary importance in moving a church toward its objectives. Well-organized Baptist churches have always operated from a task base. Many times church leaders have not recognized this. Sometimes the task base was not adequate for the church's mission. In some cases a church has tried to carry on more tasks than it had people, time, or resources to do. The number or statement of tasks is arbitrary. The following is a simple way of stating the tasks a church may wish to conduct continually.

• Govern the life and work of the church under the lordship of Christ.

• Engage in a fellowship of worship, witness, education, ministry, and application.

• Participate in cooperative work with other churches.

• Establish and maintain relationship with various publics.

• Provide resources for the work of the church.

• Teach persons the meaning(s) and skill for Christian living and church membership, using the Bible as the primary source.

• Train church members to perform the tasks of the church.

- Proclaim the gospel to believers and unbelievers.
- Reach persons for Christ and church membership.
- Perform the functions of the church.

3. Structuring Programs from Tasks

Only in the smallest of churches can all the tasks be done by the church as the total organization. For this reason a church organizes its work and people. Organization is the way work is divided. Some people become responsible to do certain tasks while other people are made responsible for a different set of tasks.

The beginning point in organizing is in the grouping of tasks for assignment. These groupings may be thought of in two ways: programs and services.

A *program* is a set of tasks which is of primary (direct) importance in achieving the church's objective. For example, proclaiming the gospel is directly related to the redemptive mission of the church.

A *service* is a set of tasks which is performed to give primary (direct) support to the programs. For example, the library service can give direct support to the Bible teaching program by providing books and other materials to church members.

"There is no absolute right way to group and assign tasks to programs and services. Perhaps the principle of grouping similar tasks provides the best basis for making judgments. Tasks are judged to be similar when they have a common purpose in such things as type of work to be done, location of work, people to be served, work processes required, equipment or materials used, or sequence of actions to be taken." [4] The important thing is to be able to make well-defined assignments.

The authority to decide tasks to be performed, programs to be conducted, and organizations to be established rests in the congregation. Baptists believe in a congregational form of church government. They follow the process of majority rule. Recommendations should be constructed from sound information and by informed leaders. The church should reserve the act of final approval on matters related to the following tasks:

---

[4] W. L. Howse and W. O. Thompson, *A Church Organized and Functioning* (Nashville: Convention Press, 1963), p. 31.

• Govern the life and work of the church under the lordship of Christ.

• Determine the church's programs, program services, and administrative services.

• Establish organization to conduct and/or coordinate programs and services.

• Determine the church's cooperative work with other churches.

• Establish and maintain appropriate external relationships.

• Select pastor, staff, and volunteer leaders, and assign responsibilities.

• Provide and allocate resources for the total work of the church.

Many Baptist churches have operated for years with several programs. The list below shows the programs a church may establish and the tasks these programs can be responsible to perform. The tasks and terminology are those which will be found in materials offered churches by the Sunday School Board, Brotherhood Commission, and Woman's Missionary Union. A careful study will reveal changes that permit these programs, and churches which establish them, to operate more effectively. The remaining chapters of this book will give detailed consideration to each program. Particular notice should be given to the fact that the program names are not necessarily organizational names. Organization is not discussed in this text, but will be presented in manuals especially prepared for each organization.

Pastoral Ministries

—Proclaim the gospel to believers and unbelievers.

—Lead the church to engage in a fellowship of worship, witness, education, ministry, and application.

—Lead the church in performing its tasks.

—Care for the church's members and other persons in the community.

Bible Teaching

—Teach the biblical revelation.

—Reach persons for Christ and church membership.

—Perform the functions of the church within its constituency.

—Provide and interpret information regarding the work of the church and the denomination.

Missions

—Teach missions.

—Engage in mission actions.

—Support world missions through praying and giving.

—Provide and interpret information regarding the work of church and the denomination.

Music

—Teach music.

—Train persons to sing, play, and lead music.

—Provide music in the church and community.

—Provide and interpret information regarding the work of church and the denomination.

Church Training

—Orient church members.

—Train church members to perform functions of the church.

—Train church leaders.

—Teach systematic theology, Christian ethics, Christian history, and church polity and organization.

—Provide and interpret information regarding the work of the church and the denomination.

Library Service

—Provide printed and audiovisual resources.

—Promote the use of printed and audiovisual resources.

—Consult with church leaders and members in the use of printed and audiovisual resources.

Recreation Service

—Provide recreation.

—Provide consultation, leadership assistance, and resources in recreation.

Administrative Services

—Conduct studies and prepare plans for governing the life and work of the church under the lordship of Christ; administer approved plans as assigned.

—Conduct studies and prepare plans for the church's future course; administer approved plans as assigned.

—Conduct studies and prepare plans for establishing and coordinating the church's programs and services; administer approved plans as assigned.

—Conduct studies and prepare plans for establishing and maintaining the church's relationships; administer approved plans as assigned.

—Conduct studies and prepare plans for allocating the church's leadership, facilities, and financial resources; administer approved plans as assigned.

SYNERGY FOR THE SEVENTIES

New terms often create confusion. New words ought to open the door to new ideas and experiences. "Synergy" is a word that may do both. Its potential is worth the risk. The word "synergy" is constructed from two other words: synthesis and energy. The idea is that certain forces, because of their nature, can be harnessed together to produce a greater force than just the sum of all. For example, if one man can pick up two hundred pounds and another two hundred and twenty pounds, we might conclude that together they could pick up four hundred and twenty pounds. The way they harness their strength may permit them to pick up five hundred and fifty pounds.

Baptist churches have always had a lot of work going on. They have been able to pick up a sizeable portion of work when measured in terms of biblical mandates. Some churches have felt that more results could have been accomplished if the strength of the church were better harnessed.

The program structure just presented when utilized as suggested in the following chapters of this book and in program manuals increases the possibility of synergy.

How can synergy work in the seventies? Consider, for example, the critical challenge a church has to teach the Word of God to all men within its community. Imagine a situation in which the following groups of people are found: persons who do not speak English, disadvantaged persons who do not feel at home with the church's membership, and persons who like Bible study but won't come to the church building. How can the job be done?

Responsibility for the non-English group and the disadvantaged would be assumed by the missions program. The responsibility for the "won't come" group would be assumed by the Bible teaching program. Because the Sunday School leaders have experience in curriculum, they could select and procure appropriate study materials. The church training program should be able to offer superior training experiences to workers because it specializes in training. The music program through special performances could be used to add color and attractiveness to the projects. The library service could supply additional resources for more effective communication by teachers or special helps for the learners.

What should be the result? The work of the church should be done with a minimum of operational folderol. The groups needing the Bible study should be afforded a tailor-made experience. The experience should be better because of the combined know-how of the programs. The experience should be more attractive because of the specialties of the music program and the library service. Each program adding what it can do best should make the whole experience better than if each worked alone. The added plus of specialized programs working together is synergy. This plus value can make a great difference to churches that set up distinct programs and then operate them to obtain their greatest contribution.

Another illustration is the critical need for a ministry to families. Families need knowledge on how to live and grow together. They need materials to guide them as they develop their understanding and concern. Families need personal attention in time of crises. Parents need special training in how to express their Christian calling as parents. Children and youth need help from churches as they prepare for marriage. Husbands and wives need help in fulfilling their responsibilities to each other.

When one considers all these needs, he can understand why churches have generally had an inadequate ministry to families. How can a church ever do an effective work? The answer is by rightly relating programs which have specific responsibility for meeting one or more of these needs. The Bible teaching program can teach more and better than any other program about the place of the family in God's plan. It can provide home materials for special guidance and leisure use by a family in its worship and education activities. It can add its support to that of pastoral ministries in time of crisis. The church training program can offer a greater variety of training projects for parents. In-depth activities which involve children with parents can be conducted. Add to these special premarital training for youth and specific training for solving common marital problems and a church can begin to obtain positive results. Include with these things family materials offered by the library service and family oriented schedules developed by the church council. Each program working together and doing what it can do best will result in a synergistic ministry with a plus contribution to solving family problems.

Can this be? Increasingly, materials specially developed by denominational agencies for church programs will have the possibility for synergy built in. A church which can identify priority needs, establish sound structures, and develop competent leaders and workers can cause these things to happen.

The adventure grows even more exciting when the variety of talents and skills of persons are synergistically combined. Baptist churches are people's churches. Just as New Testament churches had members from all walks of life, so do our churches today. The early churches combined the talents of tradesmen, politicos, scholars, professionals, uneducated, wealthy, and poor people to change the course of history. They combined their efforts toward a single objective and accomplished it in the name of Christ. A synergy of talents today can provide churches the means to shape the seventies into a decade that glorifies God and achieves his purpose.

Neither structure nor synergy can assure victory to churches in the seventies. This will come through the Spirit of Christ. Churches must seek to work where Christ is. How long has it

been since your church marveled at his presence? How long has
it been since your church realized that Christ's Spirit brings
life, hope, and love to lifeless, hopeless, and loveless men? Church
people must not fear to feel again the presence of the Lord. We
must not tremble at the thought of the Holy Spirit being
a partner in our work. We must not be ashamed to declare
the miracle of his personal presence.

The Lord said: "Where two or more are gathered together in
my name, there will I be also."

The presence of Christ molded the 120 disciples into a mighty
force at Pentecost. In that single event the Lord began a
movement that surged triumphantly across the streets of Jerusalem, the hills of Judea, the mountains of Samaria, the cities
of Asia Minor, and the uttermost parts of the world. The victory
at first was a people victory not a geographical victory. The
people of the seventies need for churches to triumph again.
Churches can triumph again. Not by structure or synergy alone
but by the power of the head of the churches, Jesus Christ.

4. Pastoral Ministries of a Church

"Pastoral ministries" is a new term which expresses concepts as old as the New Testament. Once understood and accepted, it will give each church a sense of wholeness and a healthy response to the leadership of the pastor, deacons, and staff members.

The demands of a complex society cause church members to need more assistance in meeting personal needs than ever before. To desire conversions and additions to the church assumes an equally strong desire to minister to the converts' personal needs. Such a complete ministry calls for a sharing of what has been almost entirely the work of a pastor. This complete ministry requires leadership skills and activities not required previously. The church of the future must give more attention to the personal needs of its members. It is not enough to have names on a church roll. A church must be organized and led to do more for people than ever before.

A pastor must share this ministry with such persons as deacons and staff members if the needs of members are met. This concept is not in conflict with the excellent work being done by volunteer workers in church program organizations. But it goes beyond what most workers are prepared and equipped to do.

A church today must have effective overall guidance, care, and leadership. This is what pastoral ministries provides.

A NEW TESTAMENT CONCEPT

What Jesus said and did provides a pattern for pastoral ministries. Church leaders in the first century sought to follow his example in ministering to their world.

The words of Jesus "The Son of man is come to seek and to save that which was lost" (Luke 19:10) are interpreted by another announcement, "I am come that they might have life, and that they might have it more abundantly" (John 10:10). *To save* is expressed in terms of from and to. Jesus saves *from* spiritual death and its tragic waste. W. J. McGlothlin emphasized the other side of the picture by saying he saves *to* "the soundest, fullest, completest life that is possible for each individual." [1]

When Jesus began his public ministry, he identified his mission by reading from Isaiah's prophecy: "The Spirit of the Lord is upon me, because . . . he hath sent me to heal the brokenhearted, to preach deliverance to the captives, and recovering of sight to the blind, to set at liberty them that are bruised, to preach the acceptable year of the Lord" (Luke 4:18–19). This mission required the giving of his life. Thus he fulfilled his role as shepherd and servant.

When the earthly ministry of Jesus came to a close, his work became the work of his followers. The young church of Acts 6 was experiencing the aftereffects of Pentecost. The number of disciples was growing rapidly, but success was accompanied by problems.

One of the problems was expressed in the murmuring of the Greek widows, who thought that the Hebrew widows were receiving better treatment in the church's distribution of food and other supplies. To solve the problem, the apostles exercised their role of administrative leadership as readily as they exercised their leadership in preaching.

The apostles could have reacted one of three ways: (1) ignore the complaints of the widows, declaring that the church's only

---

[1] W. J. McGlothlin, *A Vital Ministry* (New York: Fleming H. Revell Co., 1913), p. 11.

concern was in preaching the word of God; (2) give themselves completely to establishing a welfare program, thus decreasing their effectiveness in preaching; or (3) involve additional people in the task of ministering.

The apostles called the church together, presented the problem, and recommended that the third course of action be followed. To them it was obvious that both preaching and caring for human need were important. The recommendation pleased the people, and they chose seven qualified persons to help the church meet the needs. Effective preaching continued. The fellowship was preserved, and it grew. Physical and material needs were met as the result of unselfish sharing and careful administration. The apostles' leadership role was given a new dimension.

The leaders of the Jerusalem church set an example in proclaiming the gospel, maintaining fellowship, providing wise leadership, and caring for persons.

A CONTEMPORARY CONCERN

Today church members are being reminded of the scope of concern and the responses to concern revealed in the New Testament. They are asking questions about conditions in their society which need changing and the effectiveness of the gospel in bringing about these changes. This questioning is not to doubt the truth or value of the gospel revealed in the Bible through the Holy Spirit. Neither does it minimize the need of man for repentance and faith or the use of man in the proclamation of the gospel. These doctrines are changeless.

Church members want to know whether the pastoral ministries of their church is adequate for today and tomorrow. What are some indications that church members have special needs which their churches should plan to meet?

1. Emphasis on Personal Identity

Individuals trapped in the masses are saying: "Look at me!" "Listen to me!" "Care about me!" They are hoping to see the church demonstrate the claim Christ made to his disciples: "I will make you to become . . ." (Mark 1:17).

Pastoral ministries should develop the ability to relate persons to persons and persons to significant Christian activity in a way that will help the persons "become" as well as perform the essential church tasks. Persons have different needs. Their needs are met through different types of activities. This challenges the church to recognize their differences in the programs it plans and promotes.

2. Rediscovery of the Whole Person

Pastoral ministries needs to be concerned about all of man's needs: physical, mental, emotional, spiritual, and social. Pastoral ministries alone cannot meet all the needs of all men. But pastoral ministries must be a means of leading all church members to become involved in meeting needs in the most important areas of life. Pastoral ministries must seek to develop a working relation with all the helping forces in society.

3. Growth of the Inquisitive Mind

Churches are confronting an inquisitive generation that is saying, "Don't just give me your answers; help me to think!" Jesus encouraged the inquisitive mind. He challenged his hearers to think and reach some conclusions that call for commitment.

Dynamic churches need leaders in ministry who can encourage the inquisitiveness of a seeker. This is not to question the finality of Bible truths. Rather, it is to recognize that every new experience of man and every new challenge to his commitments must be examined in light of the truths revealed in the Bible.

4. Changing Sociological Patterns

Many of the approaches that churches have traditionally used to accomplish their mission have proved inadequate in today's highly mobilized world. The mission of the church in this kind of world cannot be accomplished completely by meetings in the church building. Meeting together for worship, preaching, fellowship, and teaching is essential and is the first step in being ready to minister to others. Pastoral ministries must lead churches to analyze the challenges to church attendance. Some of these challenges may be seen in the growing mobility of the family, the numerous forms of entertainment, changing work schedules, increasing leisure that permits families to take frequent weekend vacations, and the development of apartment living that is often related to a desire to be isolated.

Wallace Denton in his book *What's Happening to Our Families?* identifies one of the major challenges confronting tomorrow's church as "exploring new ideas with reference to ministering to families. A need for most church programs is for them to be more family or person-centered rather than program-centered. The family, with its pronounced areas of conflict and growing potential for strength, offers a challenge to the church not extended to any other organization in the community to make this life more abundant." [2]

These developments, and others that are as much a part of our society, demand that pastoral ministries helps the church be flexible in its approaches for communicating the gospel and caring for persons.

PASTORAL MINISTRIES TASKS

"Pastoral" is a shepherding term which focuses on the shepherd's task of caring for sheep by feeding, guiding, leading, protecting, and sheltering them. J. Lyn Elder said: "When used in connection with ministry, pastoral—though it has other meanings such as guiding and protecting—primarily means feeding or nourishing . . . and the idea of feeding, if we extend it still further has the meaning of development or growth. The shepherd, though he may care for his sheep in a compassionate sense, feeds them not just as an expression of sentiment but that they grow and be productive." [3] The nature of pastoral ministries is illustrated most clearly in the relationship of persons in the church who help one another grow and become spiritually productive.

The word "ministries" also refers to a specific kind of personal relationship. A person has a ministering relationship when he helps someone understand himself and develop fellowship with

---

2 Wallace Denton, *What's Happening to Our Families?* (Philadelphia: Westminster Press, 1963), pp. 209–12.

3 J. Lyn Elder, "Helping People in the Church, an Outline of Pastoral Care," unpublished syllabus, prepared for class use at Golden Gate Baptist Theological Seminary, Mill Valley, California.

God and man. Ministry is performed when a person acts toward another in a way that helps to meet spiritual, social, physical, mental, or emotional needs.

Every believer in Christ has ministering responsibilities. There is a sense in which a Christian is both sheep and shepherd. "Am I my brother's keeper?" is as relevant today as it was when Cain asked the question.

A church looks to the pastor for leadership that will equip individuals for ministry and will result in the best organization of groups of individuals for the church's work. Most churches have deacons who can work with the pastor in this equipping and enabling role. Many churches employ staff members who provide leadership as they are assigned responsibilities in pastoral ministries.

A church should consider adding staff members when it has needs that cannot be met by the leadership resources already available in the church. Persons in the church may lack the time or skills required for effective leadership.

The pastor leads the deacons and staff members as they provide leadership requested by the church. The pastor provides supervisory leadership and counsel for the staff and inspirational leadership and counsel for the deacons.

What does the pattern of the early church and the needs of the contemporary church suggest as tasks the church can assign to pastoral ministries? What leadership do the pastor, staff members, and deacons provide? There are four tasks that seem essential to successful pastoral ministries in a church: (1) proclaim the gospel to believers and unbelievers; (2) lead the church to engage in a fellowship of worship, witness, education, ministry, and application; (3) lead the church in performing its tasks; and (4) care for the church's members and other persons in the community. These tasks have an interdependent relationship. The adequate performance of one task helps make for success in the performance of the others.

The scope of these pastoral ministries tasks underscores the need for a pastor to share leadership with others. In addition to deacons and staff members there are other church members who have particular skills who may be called on to extend the pastoral ministries in a church.

1. Proclaim the Gospel to Believers and Unbelievers

Pastoral ministries is responsible for leading the church in proclaiming the good news about the person and the work of Jesus Christ so that persons will respond to him. Those who lead are expected to develop skills to achieve maximum effectiveness as proclaimers. They seek to lead all church members to become proclaimers to the extent of their ability and opportunity. They seek to discover and use all possible avenues in communicating the gospel.

The gospel may be proclaimed through public presentations, private conversations, written communications. The presentation of the gospel before an assembly of persons or by means of media such as radio or television is public proclamation. Preaching sermons, observing the ordinances, presenting the gospel in music, sharing personal testimonies, reading the Scriptures, presenting religious drama and films are some of the ways to proclaim the gospel to groups of persons.

Pastoral ministries assists church program organizations in proclaiming activities, such as worship experiences in Vacation Bible School and at special camps and retreats.

In addition to these, proclamation activities may be conducted in special meetings in public auditoriums. Churches may proclaim the gospel by conducting noon-day meetings in theater buildings and other places in the business center of the city. Special programs in such public places are often conducted during the Easter season. They may be continued throughout the year.

Opportunities may be found to proclaim the gospel publicly by looking for places where groups normally assemble. This is done by many churches at Christmas when the Christmas story is presented in music and drama at shopping centers and other gathering places. This method may be used at other times of the year as well. The wall of a shopping center building can serve as a screen for projecting appropriate films for family members who wait in shopping center parking lots. Parks and recreation centers offer opportunities for cooperation with a church's mission program in proclaiming the gospel. One major motel chain is offering the use of its facilities for weekly worship services for the traveling public.

Church missions and chapels need the leadership of persons who can present the gospel effectively. The need for more preaching stations is obvious in the midst of shifting and growing populations.

There are more opportunities for proclamation and needs for proclaimers in every community than pastors or other professional church leaders can meet. Their training and experience should qualify them to be the most able proclaimers, but circumstances do not permit them to be used exclusively. Deacons should be trained to work with the pastors in the task of proclamation. As these men serve effectively, they will inspire and enable others to join the ranks of those who proclaim through public presentations.

(1) *Private conversation.*—Pastoral ministries proclaims the gospel as efforts are made in private conversations to lead persons to faith in Jesus Christ. The gospel is proclaimed in counseling as persons are led to grow in the application of the gospel to specific problem areas in their lives.

Deacons have a continuing opportunity for proclamation through personal witnessing as they visit in homes of church families and when they help family members grow in understanding and in applying the gospel as a family and as individuals. In *The Ministry of the Deacon,* Howard B. Foshee suggests the Deacon-led Spiritual Care Program as a base for accomplishing this kind of ministry to families.

(2) *Written communication.*—Pastoral ministries should discover and develop opportunities to announce the gospel in written forms.

Many churches use daily newspapers only as a tool for inviting people to activities at the church. In one metropolitan area, the churches of an association combined their resources and presented the gospel in a series of attractive articles on fundamentals of our faith. These articles reached people who did not attend church.

Pastoral ministries should work with the public relations committee in securing the assistance of persons in the community who are qualified to present the gospel so that it will be communicated effectively. People who will not respond to the newspaper's invitation to come to a church gathering may read the gospel message *attentively* in their home or office and become receptive to the church's interest in them.

Tracts which present the gospel offer opportunities for proclamation. Pastoral ministries should lead the church to train persons in the effective use of tracts. A booth at a fair may provide a setting for fair-goers to read while they rest a few minutes. Concerned Christians in the booth may find opportunities to interpret the message of a tract to those who read it.

Letter-writing is another way to proclaim the gospel to groups and to individuals. New Testament letters were written to help persons and churches understand and apply the gospel. Personal letters reach persons who cannot be visited. These letters support and enforce personal witnessing. A young man in military service, a student in school, or a person who has moved away from the neighborhood are some persons who can be reached with the gospel proclaimed in a letter.

In addition to the use of daily newspaper, tracts, and personal letters, pastoral ministries should discover and develop the proclamation potential in brochures, flyers, inserts, bulletins, and church newspapers.

2. Lead the Church to Engage in a Fellowship of Worship, Witness, Education, Ministry, and Application

This task involves the development and maintenance of an intimate bond of fellowship which unites church members and makes worship, witness, education, ministry, and application natural and effective. Church members experience this fellowship as they share in a common commitment to Christ and one another. This fellowship cannot be devised or generated by church activities. Favorable conditions in church relationships tend to encourage the development and maintenance of koinonia, or Christian fellowship.

Pastoral ministries seeks to develop and maintain fellowship in the church.

Pastoral ministries helps a church develop an environment conducive to fellowship.

Pastoral ministries can help develop a regenerate and responsible church membership. Koinonia grows out of a common commitment to Christ. All the programs of a church should emphasize the importance of becoming a new creature in Christ before becoming a member of a church.

Persons who have experienced the new birth should be made aware of the nature of the fellowship of the church. The church covenant and the constitution and bylaws should state clearly how church members relate to one another. Pastoral ministries should lead the church to develop these instruments and use them effectively.

Pastoral ministries can help church members understand Christ-like concern for others. The caring task in the program of pastoral ministries is vitally related to fellowship. Caring actions both demonstrate and develop koinonia in a church.

The life of Christ is the story of demonstrated concern for the life of man. Christ desired wholeness, fulness, and maturity. Men were called to be reconciled to God, to themselves, and to their fellowmen. Christ became involved in the struggles of men whose lives were fractured, empty, and incomplete.

Unselfish concern for persons needs to be demonstrated by pastoral ministries. Christ's example and the church members' opportunity should be emphasized in all the proclaiming activities. A church should provide study of Christ's concern and should train members to develop skills for putting concern into action.

Pastoral ministries provides opportunities and encourages church members to share their needs as well as their personal resources with one another. This may be accomplished in congregational services, in organizational meetings, in deacon family care activities, in small groups that form around common interests and concerns.

Pastoral ministries can help a church develop and use standards that assist in maintaining fellowship. Inadequate communication creates misunderstandings that destroy fellowship. Guidelines are helpful in communicating a church's interest. In addition to a church covenant and a constitution and bylaws, a church should be led to adopt a statement of policies and procedures, staff position descriptions, and duties of officers and committees. These statements, properly prepared, adopted, and followed, help a church avoid disruptive conflicts.

Pastoral ministries can help a church give attention to church discipline. There will be few problems in discipline if there is a regenerate and responsible church membership, a spirit of Christ-like concern for others, and adequate criteria and tools for communicating a church's interest.

Even when these conditions exist, problems may develop in a church fellowship that need the restorative discipline Paul describes in Galatians 6:1. Pastoral ministries should seek restoration with patience and persistence. Deacons who possess the qualifications set forth in Acts 6 and in 1 Timothy 3 are particularly qualified to aid in restoring such persons to the fellowship. Their continuing relationship of concern with families in the church further qualifies them for this ministry.

In rare cases, the best action for all individuals concerned may be that which is described by Jesus in Matthew 18:15–17 and by Paul in 1 Corinthians 5. This action results in the separation of an unreconcilable person from the fellowship of the church in an effort to help him find fellowship with God that will be expressed in fellowship with man.

3. Lead the Church in Performing Its Tasks

A church assigns to pastoral ministries the leadership role in getting basic church tasks performed. This leadership involves helping the church determine the programs it needs and helping the church conduct its programs. As the need for professional leadership increases, a church may employ persons who will provide leadership in specialized programs of the church. Effective leadership in a church requires motivation, demonstration, and administration.

The focus of the leadership task is on persons. Organizations exist to meet the needs of persons. Pastoral ministries should approach this leadership role with primary concern for persons and personal relationships. This means leading the church to recognize the role of each member and to provide for relationships and activities that produce the greatest personal and corporate benefits. The accomplishment of this task requires the best use of administrative skills.

Pastoral ministries leads the church to provide for planning, conducting, and evaluating its activities. This is accomplished as the church conducts effective business meetings and provides for a functioning church council and organizational councils. Officers and committees of the church plan, conduct, and evaluate assigned areas of work. The church should be led to plan for the future through short-range and long-range planning.

Pastoral ministries leads the church to discover and secure the proper relationship of persons to tasks. The church should be led to conduct a talent survey of the church membership. Pastoral ministries should work to create a climate in which workers may be enlisted and trained. As deacons visit regularly with church families, they can discover prospective workers and report them to the appropriate persons.

Pastoral ministries provides for adequate communication with church members. Effective communication is essential to successful administration. Church staff meetings and councils provide opportunities for effective communications. The church paper, bulletins, inserts, bulletin boards, letters, as well as the direct visual and verbal contact in congregational services, are avenues along which effective communication may flow. Numerous personal contacts on the part of the pastoral ministries leaders provide opportunities for interpreting the actions of church leaders and other church members. Pastoral ministries should assist in establishing adequate means of communication and in keeping all channels clear.

Pastoral ministries inspires responsible participation in the work of the church. In personal ways—a letter, a visit in the home, a phone call—and in public expressions that are seen in print or heard in public gatherings, pastoral ministries encourages the commitment of fellow church members. Wise leaders are generous in commendation which is deserved and are careful to form a constructive relationship with those whose performance does not yet merit commendation.

4. Care for the Church's Members and Other Persons in the Community

A church should be known as a community of believers that expresses the love of Christ to persons in need. Pastoral ministries seeks the involvement of all church members in individual and group expressions of concern. Pastoral ministries recognizes that many of the needs of persons can be met through the caring actions of church program organizations. The church expresses its care when Bible teaching classes minister to the needs of persons and as mission action groups reach out to help groups of persons. There are needs that require more human, physical, and financial resources than one organization can provide. There are needs that call for the skills which leaders in pastoral ministries are expected to possess or develop. They use their skills in meeting needs that because of their complex or delicate nature require their attention. They lead the church in organizing its resources and making them available for meeting human needs but do not assume any responsibilities which can be cared for by church organizations.

A church recognizes the basic need man has to be in fellowship with God, but it knows also that man has many other needs—physical, mental, emotional, social that call for help from persons who care. Leadership in this task requires specific actions on the part of pastoral ministries.

Pastoral ministries must help church members experience a healthy regard for others and an awareness of the problems of others. Meaningful actions grow out of awareness. Jesus emphasized the importance of having a healthy regard (love) for others and for self.

Congregational services should help persons experience a healthy regard and honest awareness of others. Some churches give a major part of their mid-week services to share concern for persons with specific needs which call for caring actions, and they seek ways to meet those needs. Pastoral ministries leads the church to provide organizations in which the biblical revelation is studied and persons are led to understand Christian ethics. Counseling with individuals and groups provides opportunities for helping persons grow in concern for others.

Pastoral ministries helps the church develop and organize its resources to help persons. A church should provide for an available supply of financial and material resources and adopt a plan for administering them. A church should maintain a cooperative relationship with community agencies. It should explore the possibility of cooperative ministries with other churches.

In addition to being prepared to meet crisis situations as they are discovered, pastoral ministries should lead the church to survey the membership and community, discover personal and family needs, and provide resources for meeting them. One such survey led a church to provide a day care program for elderly persons who were left at home alone all day while all other family members worked or attended school. Facilities were provided in the church's educational building, and leaders were enlisted and trained. Elderly, often feeble, persons were rescued from loneliness and the dangers related to being left alone all day.

Pastoral ministries should involve concerned persons in ministering to others. As pastoral ministries counsels with individuals and small groups, needs are discovered that can best be met by others in the church. The needs of some can be met by a Bible class or mission action group. Referring persons to such a group does not sever the counseling relationship or indicate a lack of interest. It draws on the best resources available to enlarge the ministry to a person with needs. Where there are persons in the church membership who have particular skills that are needed to meet particular problems, their help should be enlisted. Referral can often be made to such skilled persons in areas of need such as vocational guidance and family crises.

Referral may be made to appropriate persons and agencies in the community whose resources are needed to bring help to individuals. Pastoral ministries should know the available resources in the community and keep the channels of communication open. Pastoral ministries should cooperate with those in the healing professions, in other churches and denominations, and in other agencies and institutions in order that the total resources of the community be made available to persons who need them.

This cooperation in the community further challenges pastoral ministries to lead the church to become creative in the use of its properties to meet personal and community needs. In this manner the church can receive the best dividend from the money invested in properties.

Bibliotherapy—guidance in the solution of personal problems through directed reading—can be used effectively in pastoral care. Counselors can make available the printed materials that relate to specific needs.

The accomplishment of all these actions—stimulating concern and awareness, organizing church resources, and involving persons in caring activities—will be determined by the extent of the concern and the willingness to find ways to meet needs that is possessed by leaders in pastoral ministries.

Pastoral ministries has been the work of the church since its beginning. Wise and dedicated leaders in pastoral ministries can help the church continue to do its work with vitality.

When a church entrusts to its pastor the weighty responsibility for leadership in pastoral ministries, it is demonstrating a confidence and pledging a response. For the pastor, and others who are enlisted to serve with him in pastoral ministries, this is an awesome responsibility and a challenging trust. It calls for the best leadership that dedicated, trained, and growing leaders can give.

5. A Church in Bible Study and Outreach

The heart of a church's corporate work, like the personal work of a Christian, is to find and do the will of God in today's world.

To find the will of God, a church must keep within communication range of God.

People do not have to be ignorant about any vital matter concerning God, his purpose in the world, or his expectancies of man. God has made these things unmistakably clear in the Scriptures. If churches today would discover the mind of God, they must search the Bible.

THE BIBLE PROVIDES THE MESSAGE TO BE SHARED

The message to be shared involves a person, an action, and a proclamation. The person of Jesus Christ is central in the message. The action, what God did in Christ for man, is the gospel—the good news. Paul described it in these words: "I delivered unto you first of all that which I also received, how that Christ died for our sins according to the scriptures; and that he was buried, and that he rose again the third day according to the scriptures" (1 Cor. 15:3–4). Proclamation and witness are the Christian's part in carrying out the redemptive purpose of God. This is the only incomplete action in the story of redemption. All is now ready for lost man's response.

IN THE BIBLE GOD REVEALS THE MEANS OF SPREADING THE GOOD NEWS

The means God prescribes for proclaiming the gospel is really simple: tell it and *live* it. The method is verbal—the story must be told. The setting for the story is the life of the messenger. The message must also be lived, and it must be lived in the world.

At this point two commands to Christians may seem to contradict each other. One says "be separate" and another says "go into the world." Both of these commands are binding. We can never fulfil our evangelistic mission in isolation. There is a delicate balance to be maintained. We must not separate ourselves from the people to whom the message is to be proclaimed.

A REDEEMED HUMANITY IS IN THE MIND OF GOD

God created the world, and man is his highest creation. Man was made a living soul with mind and will. Man sinned and broke fellowship with God. From the beginning of the separation, God has continually sought man's redemption. The Bible reveals God's plan to redeem his lost creation.

Would a church know the mind of God? Would God's people let his plan guide their lives? Then teach the Bible. Therein is revealed the mind and the will of God. Here is the open door for the leadership of his Holy Spirit.

PROVIDE A BROADER BASE FOR BIBLE TEACHING

Jesus Christ was a teacher. One of his major approaches in accomplishing his purpose in the world was teaching. "And Jesus, when he came out, saw much people, and was moved with compassion toward them, because they were as sheep not having a shepherd: and he began to teach them many things" (Mark 6:34). Jesus Christ is recognized as Master Teacher by Christian and secular educators alike.

Christ expects his church to teach. The familiar commission

given to the church culminates in teaching which leads to fulfilling the work of Christ. Jesus called his followers disciples. Disciples are learners, and learning is an educational experience. Disciples are to be taught to observe all that Jesus commanded about worshiping God, witnessing to men, learning the Christian faith, ministering to the needs of persons, and applying the Christian faith in every aspect of daily life. Here is something of the gigantic work a church is to do.

The major issues confronting the world today are a concern to the Christian in his total assignment. They are significant for one who would follow Christ. From time to time, certain aspects of life come to the surface, demanding immediate and urgent attention. This is obvious in many of the great social issues of the day. Application in daily life is the natural expression of genuine Christian experience. James wrote: "But someone will say, 'You have faith and I have actions." My answer is, 'Show me how you can have faith without actions; I will show you my faith by my actions'" (James 2:18, TEV).[1]

Paul understood the place of teaching in a New Testament church. In Ephesians 4 Paul spoke of the various calls and assignments of Christ. Some are to be apostles; some, prophets; some, evangelists; some, pastors and teachers. The educational approach is clearly identified. Teaching shares with other work in the full ministry of the Word and in the purpose of the churches. Paul described the educational assignment when he spoke of "the perfecting of the saints, for the work of the ministry, for the edifying of the body of Christ: till we all come in the unity of the faith, and of the knowledge of the Son of God, unto a perfect man, unto the measure of the stature of the fulness of Christ" (Eph. 4:12–13). Leading men into a clear understanding of the revelation of God in the Bible must be a priority concern in the churches.

1. Enlarge the Concept of Sunday School

The term "Sunday School" has been used for generations as the name for the organized Bible teaching program of a

---

1 *Good News for Modern Man: The New Testament in Today's English Version,* © copyright American Bible Society, 1966. This and all other quotations from this version are used by permission.

church. It is not necessary to change this time-honored name. Some universities, retaining their chartered names, have extended themselves beyond their campuses and regularly scheduled classes. In a similar way in our churches, Sunday School is being extended into a comprehensive Bible teaching program. A church cannot provide all the Bible teaching that is needed in a Sunday program alone.

A church's task is not simply to have Sunday School but to reach persons and teach them the record of God's revelation. This calls for imagination and a spirit of conquest.

2. Multiply Approaches to Bible Study

In looking to the seventies, it becomes increasingly necessary to provide many approaches to the study and teaching of the Bible. Not all the persons who ought to be reached for Bible study by a church can or will come to the church building for this experience. There are many facets of the Bible teaching program which will greatly extend the reach of the churches in the days ahead. Consider these approaches:

(1) *Sunday School.*—The Sunday sessions will continue to be the major approach of the Bible teaching program. A Sunday School consists of ongoing, age-graded Bible classes meeting on Sunday morning or, in some mission situations, on Sunday afternoon. Another phase of the Sunday School consists of Bible study groups meeting during the week for those who cannot attend on Sunday. Many Sunday workers or shift workers need this opportunity if they are to participate.

(2) *Extension Bible study activities.*—In addition to the basic approach made through the Sunday School, a church may want to provide one or more of the following extension or "extended" Bible study activities:

The *Vacation Bible School* is a major facet of the Bible teaching program of a church. However, it is more than a part of the Bible teaching program. The Vacation Bible School shares the four tasks of the Bible teaching program, and, in addition, performs tasks for other church programs as it:

- Teaches music
- Teaches persons to lead, sing, and play music
- Provides music in the church and community

- Trains church members to perform the functions of the church; and teaches Christian theology, Christian ethics, Christian history, and church polity
- Teaches missions
- Performs mission action

Vacation Bible School is age-graded and is conducted during vacation time, offering from twelve to thirty or more hours of curriculum devoted to study and action in the areas mentioned.

The Bible teaching program should also include mission Vacation Bible Schools in areas where new churches are needed. These may be, and are designed to be, the means of starting new churches.

An increasing number of churches are already including *Weekday Bible Study* in their Bible teaching program. This is an ongoing age-graded Bible course (usually thirty, fifty-minute sessions) with emphasis, primarily, on historical and chronological Bible study. It meets sometime other than Sunday. Specially designed courses of study are used. Though Weekday Bible Study has no action program, its members are encouraged to participate in Sunday School and in other programs. This facet of the Bible teaching program adds a depth study which makes the Sunday sessions more rewarding.

Bible conferences offer a new and challenging potential for most churches. The term "Bible conferences" means a series of sessions devoted to the study of any portion or portions of the Bible. Bible conferences major on study of the Bible and are appropriate whenever church leaders feel they should be conducted. These sessions call for the use of appropriate learning aids and participation on the part of those in attendance. The Bible conferences should not duplicate the Sunday School course but may in some instances be designed to support it. When Bible conferences enlist persons not enrolled in Sunday School, participants are encouraged to become active members of the Sunday School and other programs.

The approach offered through Bible conferences will enable a church to strengthen the curriculum at various points where special needs exist. This is particularly true where more depth Bible study is desired along doctrinal and topical lines. For example, the Sunday School curriculum may cover in two or three lessons a passage such as the Beatitudes. Led by the pastor or some other

Bible scholar, an intensive, depth study of Matthew 5–7 would be of great value.

Many churches are offering Bible study opportunities through *Fellowship Bible Classes* and may call these Neighborhood Bible Classes. These Bible study groups are usually of a short-term nature. They meet in homes or apartments for the purpose of involving unreached persons in Bible study with the view of reaching them for membership in the "home" Sunday School and the church. In some instances, these classes may be and can be used as the means of establishing a new church. Study may be based on a specially designed curriculum or on the current Sunday School curriculum.

The *Bible study course* is a plan of study based on the resources and requirements of the New Church Study Course. It may include such approaches as special weeks of study (January Bible Study), individual home study, programed instruction, study in retreat or camp settings, preview studies, or the Bible Survey Plan. There are many resources now available and others will be forthcoming.

There is urgent need for reenforcing the family as a teaching unit. Some immediate ways this need can be met partially are: through Adult assembly programs, special meetings with parents and teachers, making special applications of lessons to parents as teachers of their children.

With the population increasing and many new communities being established, *new Sunday Schools* are required. Establishing a new Sunday School in an area where a church is needed with the intent of its becoming a church is a major responsibility of the Bible teaching program after approval by the church. The new school may begin with only one class if there are not adequate resources for a graded school.

UNDERSTAND THE BIBLE TEACHING PROGRAM

Southern Baptist churches expect their program organizations to do significant work for the church. This responsibility gives each program basic and important work to do and assures that the work of the church will be done. Ninety-nine percent of Southern Baptist churches have a Sunday School, and now use the Sunday School for heavy program responsibilities. The comprehensive teaching of the Bible undergirds all church programs. To discharge its responsibility, a Sunday School must clearly understand and implement the enlarged concept of a Bible teaching program.

Attention has already been called to many facets of the Bible teaching program. These are implemented through carrying out basic actions.

Consider now the major responsibilities of a church's Bible teaching program.

1. Teach for Decision

The story of redemption is the heart of the biblical revelation, which is the content area of the Bible-teaching program.

"Revelation in the Christian sense is that self-disclosure of God in Christ which makes it possible for man to know God and to live a life of fellowship with him . . . the record of this revelation—the literary means of its transmission to us—is the Bible." [2]

Bible study is of vital importance to two groups—Christians and unsaved persons. The biblical revelation is the foundational curriculum for a church. The task *teach the biblical revelation* means involving persons in the study of God's written revelation. "Teach" involves guidance in learning experiences.

Some continuing learning activities are:
- Exploring the content of God's written revelation
- Discovering the meaning, value, and relevance of the Bible
- Appropriating the meaning and value of the Bible
- Applying in all their relations the meaning, value, and relevance of the Bible

In the Bible we see God in his relationship to man, to his created universe, and to history. We see man as he was created (in the image of God), as he now is in his broken relationship with God through pride and disobedience (a sinner), and as he can become in redemption (a child of God, a new creation).

In the Bible we see the life, death, and resurrection of Christ as the climax of God's self-disclosure, though it was by no means the conclusion of it. The activity of the Holy Spirit in the life and work of the church was necessary to demon-

---

[2] W. T. Conner, *Christian Doctrine* (Nashville; Broadman Press, 1937), p. 27.

strate and interpret the full meaning of God's revelation through Christ.

The nature, purpose, and functions of a church progressively unfold in the New Testament writings. A church is seen as a fellowship of believers under the lordship of Christ and led by the Holy Spirit.

God included in his self-disclosure the person and work of the Holy Spirit. Although the nature and work of the Spirit may be seen throughout the Old Testament, it is only through the New Testament that his person and ministry are fully revealed. The Spirit came in power at Pentecost. He has continued to work in and through the church to convict men of sin, to interpret the revelation of God in Christ, and to be the personal guide and enabling power in the life of every believer.

The Bible is taught with the hope that persons may, through the Holy Spirit, be led to respond to God with maturing faith, love, and obedience. One is not educated into a positive response to God, but the teaching of the message of the Bible is an invaluable aid in leading one to an encounter with God through the work of the Holy Spirit.

The time of teaching is a time for decision. The response of every student of the Word should be, "Lord, what will thou have me do?"

As a church evaluates its Bible teaching program, some questions must be faced: Have the teachers been faithful and effective in teaching the message of God's Word? Have teachers understood and accepted their heavy accountability by careful preparation of heart and mind? Do teachers master the truth so that it in turn masters them? Do they set a worthy example by portraying Christian principles in their daily lives? Does the teaching of the Word find a ready response in the lives of the members—does it make a positive difference? Are the teachers and members working toward the goal of growing up into Christ in all things?

2. Focus On and Reach the Unreached

Jesus declared, "As my Father hath sent me, even so send I you" (John 20:21). He also said to his disciples, "Pray ye therefore the Lord of the harvest, that he will send forth labourers into his harvest" (Matt. 9:38). As a final commission to his followers, Jesus said: "Go ye therefore, and teach all nations, baptizing them in the name of the Father, and of the Son, and of the Holy Ghost" (Matt. 28:19). These passages constrain a church to have compassionate concern for the unreached.

An important task a church assigns to its Bible teaching program is: *reach persons for Christ and church membership.* To accomplish this task, a Bible teaching program must involve persons in Bible study, lead them to accept Christ as Lord, and lead them to express their commitment to Christ through uniting with the church. "Reach" as used in this task means enlisting, involving, or leading. The purpose of this work is to influence persons to follow the leadership of the Holy Spirit in regard to Bible study, personal relationship with Christ, and relationship to a church.

Reaching persons means enlisting and involving in Bible study unsaved persons, unchurched Christians, church members who are not a part of the Bible teaching program, and the children of these groups. This requires locating these persons geographically. Although enlistment in Bible study is not essential to becoming a Christian or uniting with a church, such enlistment is a vital part of this task and leads to its fulfilment. Demonstrating unmistakable concern for persons who need Bible study and right relationship to Christ is a basic requirement. A focus on the unreached calls for leading unsaved persons (who may or may not now be a part of the Bible teaching program) to accept Christ as Lord. It involves leading unchurched Christians (who may or may not now be a part of the Bible teaching program) to express their commitment to Christ through uniting with the church.

The actions of this task require going to the homes, businesses, or other places wherever persons may be found in need of Christ, Bible study, and church membership.

Personal ministry, witnessing, and teaching are the methods to be used by the Bible teaching program to enlist church members in Bible study, to win unsaved persons to Christ, and to lead the unchurched to unite with the church.

The unreached person must be made aware of the love and

concern of the person or persons who are seeking to win him. He must never be viewed as a statistic. He must know that he is respected as a person of worth and significance. When the person is led to study the Bible individually or in a Bible class, the Holy Spirit speaks to his needs. He may then be led to make a commitment of his life to Christ. The three stories in Luke 15 give Christ's interpretation of the essentials of a church's outreach.

Look for a moment at the setting of Luke 15 and see what situation called forth the stories. Phillips' translation provides a good perspective. "Now all the tax collectors and 'outsiders' were crowding around to hear what he had to say. The Pharisees and the scribes complained of this, remarking, 'This man accepts sinners and even eats his meals with them'" (Luke 15:1–25, Phillips) .[3]

The scribes and Pharisees had their focus on the wrong people. They saw themselves, enjoyed the blessings of God themselves, but missed the point of the gospel—that it was good news for all. So when Christ showed concern for, and gave his attention to, the sinners and "outsiders," the religionists of the time found fault with him. Their focus was wrong.

We read of the callousness of the scribes and Pharisees and are quick to see that their preoccupation with themselves and their own narrow interests closed their minds to the outgoing and inclusive love of God for all men. But what of ourselves? Where do we in our churches place the greatest emphasis? Who gets the most time of pastors, Sunday School teachers, deacons, and other church workers? Is it the lost persons, the outsiders, the uncommitted?

Evaluation reports of churches and Sunday School classes testify to a need for focusing the efforts on outreach. Sunday worship service attendance includes few unsaved persons. The same is true for Sunday School classes—the lost persons are not there. Of course, the sermon and the Sunday School lesson should be for Christians, also. The study and worship should edify the Christian, strengthen his faith, and sharpen

---

3 *The New Testament in Modern English,* © J. B. Phillips, 1958. Used with permission of the Macmillan Company.

his sensitivity to his responsibilities. But the lost person should be brought into such an environment as well.

A renewed emphasis on the outreach mission of a church at any time revives, inspires, and brings rededication and commitment to Christians. No one can share with others what he does not possess.

Outreach is the biblically based direction of concern toward unreached, unsaved, uncommitted people. It is a church's organized effort to reach persons who are immediate prospects for the church for worship, witness, education, ministry, and application. The mission action of a church (the responsibility of the Woman's Missionary Union and Brotherhood) is directed to persons of special need and circumstance who are not immediate prospects of a church.

Has your Sunday School led in reaching prospects for the church so that the church constantly is provided with a "growing edge"? Is the Sunday School enrolment growth in keeping with the number of unreached people in the community? Are there many unsaved and unchurched people enrolled in your classes, especially adults? Is there a plan for discovering prospects which is effectively functioning? Is there an up-to-date prospect file in use by all departments and classes? Are the members involved regularly in helping to locate prospects for the church? Have new classes and departments been added in keeping with the needs? Having done these things, then, has your church tried all available means of communicating the gospel to the community? Consider some of the following means.

Public news media are open to the churches. Creative awareness articles in newspapers and spot announcements on television and radio can be used not just to promote meetings but to inform the general public of a church's concerns in the community.

In some metropolitan areas it is next to impossible to get past doormen into apartment buildings. Many homes are not open to the stranger. College dormitory rules are so stringent on some campuses that personal contact with students is most difficult to achieve. In such instances, direct mail to prospects can be helpful in opening the way for later visits. Church bulletins can be mailed. Cultivation materials may be sent to prospects over a period of weeks. This mail may be followed up by telephone calls where numbers are available. All of this, if carefully planned and prayerfully conducted, could open the way for personal visits.

The key to enlisting a person is in his awareness of the member's vital personal concern. Friendly acts at appropriate times, special remembrances, teaching visits, alertness to special needs show in practical ways that the "prospect" is not a statistic but a real human being.

These few means mentioned serve only to suggest that reaching complex persons in a complex society is not a simple matter. It calls for commitment, imagination, creativity, and consistency.

3. Secure Outcomes in Action

The third, and perhaps the most difficult, task of the Bible teaching program speaks to the matter of Christian involvement in carrying out the functions of a church.

"It's not what you do; it's the spirit that counts" is only a half-truth. The letter of James makes it clear that Christians are saved to serve. He instructed Christians to take action based on their understanding of the Word. "Do not fool yourselves by just listening to his word. Instead, put it into practice. For whoever listens to the word but does not put it into practice is like a man who looks in a mirror and sees himself as he is. He takes a look at himself and then goes away, and at once forgets what he looks like. But the man who looks closely into the perfect law that sets men free, who keeps on paying attention to it, and does not simply listen and then forget it, but puts it into practice—that man will be blessed by God in what he does" (James 1:22-25, TEV).

All that the Sunday School has done in leading persons in the study of the Bible and in reaching persons for Christ and church memberships is incomplete until the members have been led to do the work of a church. Therefore, the Bible teaching program has the task of leading all church members to worship, witness, educate, minister, and apply the teachings of Jesus in all areas of life. In general, this task involves leading the members as individuals to witness and minister to any person any time and any place as opportunity offers itself. Particularly, the task involves an organized effort to direct ministry and witnessing to members of the church and of the Bible teaching program. If a Sunday School has discharged its responsibility, it already has been ministering and witnessing to immediate prospects of the church as it has sought to reach all prospects for Christ and church membership.

The members of the Bible teaching program should carry out church functions in the church building, in their own homes, in places of business, in the homes of others, or wherever they may have opportunity.

Note some essential actions and approaches of the Bible teaching program in accomplishing each of the functions of the church within its constituency.

- **Worship**

(1) Providing opportunities for groups to worship

(2) Leading church members to recognize and use opportunities and resources for worshiping individually and by families

A major contribution of the Bible teaching program to worship comes through leading persons to apprehend God's nature and will through Bible study. Effective Bible study both requires and induces worship.

Another contribution the Bible teaching program may make is through leading persons to participate in the worship services of the church. An invitation to attend Sunday School should also be an invitation to attend the worship services. The worship service should be a natural follow-up for the Bible study period.

Other group worship experiences are provided in the Sunday School sessions and in Vacation Bible School. Appropriate worship experiences in the department can be a vital part of the learning situation.

Many other special group-worship opportunities are provided for class groups, department leadership groups, clinics, spiritual preparation retreats, and neighborhood prayer groups.

A major opportunity for leading church members to worship comes in the regular study experiences of a Sunday School class. When effective Bible study takes place and persons come to understand more clearly the revelation of God, there is encounter. And worship is encounter with God. Bible study should result in hearing and heeding God's call to obedience. This, too, is worship.

Worshiping individually and worshiping by families are other areas of responsibility for the Bible teaching program. Regular family worship should be the goal of every Christian parent.

• **Witness**

(1) Providing opportunities for groups to witness

(2) Leading church members to recognize and use opportunities and resources for witnessing individually and within families

The content areas of the Bible teaching program major on the redemptive message of the Bible. Such study motivates witness. Not all of our witness is to lost people. Christians should witness to one another of the manifold grace of God and should tell others what Christ has done for them. Sunday Schools, Vacation Bible School, Weekday Bible Study groups, mission Sunday Schools, fellowship Bible classes—all provide opportunities for groups to witness.

Christians witnessing to one another build up faith and the spirit of koinonia. This creates an atmosphere for an evangelistic witness. Such sharing of rich personal experiences is a natural outcome of Bible study.

The Sunday School can provide leadership for the church in special witnessing projects such as the distribution of Bibles. Organized groups of persons or individuals may be involved in perennial evangelistic efforts that supplement and enhance the special evangelistic campaigns of the church. Distributing the Bible or portions of the Bible is a fruitful way of engaging in a witnessing activity.

Cultivative visitation, in which prospects may be assigned individually or by families, is a vital part of the total witnessing plan which may be conducted by the Sunday School. Through its organization, the Sunday School has the logical means to assign responsibility for witnessing to every person whom the church should reach. Lost persons already enrolled in Sunday School and under the teaching and preaching influence of the church are likely ready to receive a Christian witness. Un-

saved and unchurched members of the families of pupils enrolled in Sunday School, Vacation Bible School, or other ex-
tensions of the Bible teaching program are generally easier
to approach and more ready to respond to Christ. A worthy
goal of the Sunday School should be to enlist every church
member in concern that results in witnessing and thus assure
a continuing evangelistic thrust into the surrounding community.

• **Educate**

(1) Leading church members to recognize and use opportunities and resources for education individually and by families

The Bible teaching program carries special responsibility for
leading church members to recognize and use opportunities
and resources for learning individually and within families.
Such learning adds a big plus to the Bible teaching that is
done through the Sunday School and the various extension
Bible study activities. The Bible teaching program needs to help
families find appropriate resources for teaching in the home and
to provide guidance in using such materials.

A recent research project raised a question, What do Southern
Baptists consider to be the leading moral, social, or economic
problems? The respondents were asked to check from an extensive list the five problems that concerned them most. The
problem of "parental neglect of responsibility in rearing children" was checked by 73.6 percent. The next highest priority
problem, "reluctance of individuals to take a stand on moral,
social, or economic issues" was 11 percentage points below this
or 62.7 percent.

The scriptural ideal for a home is that it be a school for
Christian living. Paul recognized the contribution which was
made to Timothy, this son in the ministry, through the effective
living and teaching of the mother and grandmother.

The regular Sunday sessions can be used to interpret to parents
the responsibilities and resources for educating children in the
home. Special opportunities, such as parenthood-enrichment
meetings, alternate units of study, and teaching visits are additional avenues for education. A special officer is provided in
the new organization to magnify family ministry.

The Bible teaching program is also obligated to interpret opportunities for educating others through individual contacts. These opportunities may be interpreted and promoted in the regular meetings of the Sunday School or in special meetings as occasion requires. Opportunities for educating others through individual contacts may involve such things as sharing through personal testimonies, books, or magazines. It involves encouraging any learning which will enrich the person's relationship with Christ and helping the person to develop the full extent of his capability. This development involves the total person.

Sunday School teachers can encourage their members to engage appropriately in the study experiences offered through the other organizations of the church. A church provides many resources for learning, but a desire for learning must motivate the use of these resources. As Sunday School teachers and members study the Bible together, many opportunities emerge for stimulating within each pupil a desire to "grow up into him in all things, which is the head, even Christ" (Eph. 4:15).

• Minister

(1) Providing opportunities for groups to minister

(2) Leading church members to recognize and use opportunities and resources for ministering individually and by families

Implicit in the ministering function of a church is ministering in Jesus' name. For the Christian and a church, human need is an open door, a beckoning hand for sharing. Crucial needs may be spiritual, physical, emotional, mental, or social. Ministering in the name of Christ is desperately needed—by the needy people in the world as well as by individual Christians. Through the Bible teaching program the church may minister on a comprehensive basis to its members, their families, and immediate prospects for the church. Through the Woman's Missionary Union and Brotherhood, the mission actions of a church carry out ministries to those in special need and circumstance who are not immediate prospects for the church. Pastoral ministries of the church likewise is involved in all of these areas of ministry.

There are opportunities for groups to minister. Surveys are needed to determine where ministry is called for. These opportunities are many and urgent. Almost any church will find those among its own members and their families who are in physical need of one kind or another. There are the lonely, rejected, despondent, and discouraged. There are those in rest homes, hospitals, homes for unwed mothers, and in juvenile detention homes. There are divorcees; there are lonely students in college dormitories; there are the alcoholics; there are the widows. Some of these are members of the church. They desperately need to feel that the church cares. This must be the concern of the pastor and the church staff and, likewise, of all other members of the body of Christ. A survey of the needs for ministry would be enlightening and would serve as a strong motivation for response in service. Each of the persons in need is a call for the church membership to practice in its deepest meaning a verse learned in childhood: "Be ye kind one to another, tenderhearted, forgiving one another, even as God for Christ's sake hath forgiven you" (Eph. 4:32).

The Sunday School can use its regular contacts for discovering numerous crisis situations which call for the individual ministries of church members and sometimes may call for referral to professional help. Information about these crisis situations should be shared with the pastor.

There are opportunities for many helpful ministry projects to show love and concern for members and prospective members. Thanksgiving, Christmas, and other such special occasions in the church's calendar often may be the only time when food and other needed services are provided. There are needs for ministry to those who are temporarily away from home in military service, in college or universities, or at work. The Bible teaching program includes these continuing opportunities for Christian ministry.

In the Bible teaching program church members should be led to recognize opportunities and use resources for ministering individually and by families. These ministries would be in the nature of spontaneous ministering. Any of the regular Sunday School meetings may be used for providing and interpreting resources for ministering. Special meetings, such as churchwide vocational guidance and family ministry clinics, may be needed to offer additional help.

• **Apply**

(1) Providing opportunities for groups to apply Christian principles in all issues of everyday life

(2) Leading church members to recognize and use opportunities and resources for applying Christian principles in all issues of everyday life

In a real sense, each of the four functions already discussed involves the application of the Christian faith. However, growing out of extensive studies by the denomination's '70 Onward Committee, a fifth function of a church, "apply," has been recognized. This function refers to the practical application of Christian principles in all the issues of life.

The Christian, motivated by a knowledge of God's Word and an understanding of his purposes in the world, is concerned about expressing his Christian faith under all circumstances. As a Christian, he is deeply interested in alleviating social and moral evils. Whatever influence he has with the elected officials may be appropriately exercised. Individual involvement in campaigns to improve television programs and other entertainment media and to improve the morals of the community should be considered natural outcomes of aroused spiritual concern for the welfare of persons. These items mentioned above would be the appropriate concerns of classes or departments.

A continuing responsibility of leaders in the Bible teaching program is to lead church members to recognize opportunities and use resources for applying Christian principles in all issues of everyday life. The Christian life is not divided into the sacred and the secular. All of life is to be permeated with the Spirit of Christ.

As you evaluate progress in leading church members to do the work of the church, consider these questions: Have the leaders and members recognized that their responsibility does not end with the study of the Word, but only begins there? Are the members being personally involved in doing the work of a New Testament church? Are workers and members alike participating meaningfully in the prayer and worship services of the church? Is regular worship with the family being practiced in the homes? Is the practice of daily Bible study and prayer prevailing throughout the church? Are the church members being led to witness daily to fellow Christians and unsaved persons? Is general use being made of witnessing materials which will assist in effective witnessing? Are members of the Bible teaching program being encouraged to enrol in the study activities of the other church organizations so that learning in all areas of the church's life will be realized? Are church members being led to express their concern for persons by ministering to their needs in Jesus' name? Are they being led to look for ways they can spontaneously express the love of Christ for others through personal Christian ministry?

4. Supporting Church and Denominational Emphases

The Bible teaching program, along with other church programs, provides broad support for the major church and denominational emphases. This is done in various ways. In each case, specific emphases are related to and are vital parts of the tasks given to the organizations. For example, because of the Bible teaching program's task of witnessing, it is logical for a church to use its Sunday School in supporting revival meetings, cooperating with the mission organizations in special mission offerings, undergirding the Cooperative Program, and providing a practical means for securing pledges and receiving contributions to the church budget.

A comprehensive support of the church and denominational emphases comes through the fourth task of the Bible teaching program (shared by all church programs), *provide and interpret information regarding the work of the church and denomination.* Doing this work involves presenting either orally or in printed form and explaining the significance of factual materials concerning goals, plans, and activities of the church and denomination. This information not only involves the local church but the church as related to the association, the state convention, the Southern Baptist Convention, and the world.

What information is to be shared? *The information to be shared should be vital to the life and work of the church and/or denomination.* It should be in keeping with the church tasks performed by the Bible teaching program. And it should be

shared appropriately in keeping with the age, maturity, and
needs of the various members of the groups.

One of the responsibilities is to help the church develop
a well-informed, responsive constituency. Essential information
for all members of the church is carried through the publications of the Bible teaching program. Content and guidance
for sharing it through the various avenues are provided. An
informed Baptist is usually a cooperating Baptist.

To evaluate performance in this area, consider these questions: Has progress been made in enlisting all church members
to support the church budget and Cooperative Program? Is
the stewardship of money and of life effectively taught
throughout the year? Has support been given to the special
missions offerings, making them truly churchwide? Has special
support been given to the revival meetings held by the church,
leading out in attendance and in personal soul-winning efforts?
Has information regarding the work of the church and denomination been consistently provided and interpreted to the constituency?

ADVENTURES IN TEACHING THE WORD

This book interprets a *dynamic* church. The use of the
word "dynamic" indicates that there is movement, action, excitement—there is adventure in the dynamic church. This
chapter has been devoted, primarily, to a presentation of the
work of a church in Bible study and outreach. These two
areas of concern are at the center of the life of a New Testament church. And exciting things are happening in those
churches which are daring and imaginative in Bible teaching
and outreach.

Tallowood Baptist Church in Houston, Texas, was cramped
for space—even with dual worship services. They embarked on
an adventure with three Sunday School hours and three separate worship services. Each of these Sundays Schools has its
own faculty and enrolment—and prospects! Daring? Yes, but a
rewarding adventure in Bible study and outreach.

Consider the Northrich Baptist Church in Richardson, Texas,
that decided that their building facilities should be used every
day in teaching and reaching. Their first weekday venture was

with one kindergarten with seventeen children enrolled. (There were only four hundred church members then.) Child care was added, then came after-school activities, using Weekday Bible Study materials, *Adventure,* and other Bible-oriented materials. At the last report, that adventurous ministry had grown to include twenty-three Christian teachers ministering to 250 children five days a week—a total of forty-eight hundred hours of teaching each week!

In the Bible teaching program there is challenge, adventure, excitement, hard work, and satisfaction. It is satisfying to know that when you enrol a little child and begin to make him aware of God and the Bible, you are helping to shape the future of the child and all those he touches. To walk up to the church on Sunday morning and be greeted by a young boy who is bursting to tell you what he has brought "to help with the lesson this morning" is a satisfaction that only a teacher of boys can know. When you lovingly and firmly guide an adolescent from indifference, through doubt, to secure, contagious belief in the contemporary Christ, you feel an excitement and sense of accomplishment. The teacher who visits and enlists a young family and later counsels with them in difficulties, showing them how to find resources in God's Word, has one of life's most exciting assignments.

At every stage of his life, man needs God. He needs to be reached with the redemptive message of Jesus Christ. He needs to be shown step by step the way to grow in Christ. He needs to be led to act and work as a Christian, sharing his testimony and his concern for others. He must be ministered to in his hours of need. He must be challenged to be all that he can be in Christ. And this is the adventure we have in Bible study and outreach.

W. L. Howse in his book *Those Treasured Hours* gives a glimpse of the glorious task of teaching:

> The Bible is not an ordinary book, and no class session is an ordinary period of time. When the teacher reads the Bible, God speaks. This book is a lamp and a light. People in sin are in spiritual darkness. The Bible tells of Jesus, the Light of the world, the Saviour of mankind. The entire Bible points

to Christ, the Lord and Master of life. When one takes this library of sixty-six books into his classroom and teaches from it, he is dealing with the most unusual Book in the world, the most unusual message in the world, and is spending the most important time in the world.[4]

---

[4] Nashville: Convention Press, 1960, pp. 5–6.

6. The Church Missions Program

Christ's commission has echoed through the centuries, transcending time and outliving all eras. The commission is contemporary: "Go, then, to all peoples everywhere and make them my disciples: baptize them in the name of the Father and of the Son and of the Holy Spirit, and teach them to obey everything I have commanded you. And remember! I will be with you always, to the end of the age" (Matt. 28:19–20, TEV).

A CHURCH: WORLD RESPONSIBILITY

Christ's commission is a mandate with a world scope—all nations, even unto the end of the world. The mission he describes is the most demanding assignment ever made. Christ, who commissioned his church and gave his followers their marching orders, describes his work in the world in clear terms. The contemporary challenge is as exacting as the original one: a church must be able to take hold of its mission on Christ's scale—giving the whole gospel to the whole world.

Although from century to century the nature of world need may change, its crushing weight is constant. A church's responsibility for lifting the burden of need never subsides. Human despair gripped the mind of Christ and helped set the course of his work from day to day. In this century the human situation, together with God's mandate to disciple the nations, is the church's signal to missions advance.

The world view of need can be understood best in human terms. Everywhere are graphic parallels to the world that Jesus knew—the world of Bethesda, of Nicodemus, of Mary Magdalene, and of lonely lepers. The twentieth-century counterparts are legion: an aged patriarch in Yemen who has never seen a doctor; a modern youth in Africa, anguished by the vacuum left from his rejection of tribal religion; the hostile rebellion of an American youth, not quite sixteen, but in trouble with the law; a shy Oriental mother, bowing low to Buddha and rising with an empty heart; an old woman dying from cancer, cruelly slow to take its toll.

The circumference of a church's missions concern is the length and breadth of the world itself—with its total needs. Anything short of this weakens the redemptive nature of the gospel.

God established his church as the agency through which he would redeem the world. The late W. O. Carver, who taught missions at Southern Baptist Theological Seminary, explained the role of the church this way: "Between the lost world and the kingdom of God the Lord placed the church as a medium through which the saved labor for the salvation of the world."

Every fellowship of believers is a channel of God's redemptive purpose. Within the limits of its ability and range of influence, a church is a responsible body of witnesses charged with making the truth of God known to the whole world.

Each church must measure itself in terms of its relationship to a world task. Churches must discern what God is doing in the world and share his work in it. Every church must start where it is and ultimately expand its horizon until the scope of its interest and concern includes the world. A church's neighborhood and the world's frontier are both within a church's responsibility.

The church missions program is committed to helping a church achieve its full potential in proclaiming the changeless gospel to a changing world.

A CHURCH'S MISSIONS TASKS

A church's work in the world is a continuation of the work Christ began. A church is the body of Christ—his hands, his feet, his voice in today's world—serving the world as Christ did.

A church has two broad areas of work. A church must function to build up and strengthen its own body. A church must also reach out beyond itself to those in need of the gospel. In reaching beyond itself, a church seeks through outreach and missions to extend the message of the gospel to all persons. The object of a church's outreach is to reach immediate prospects for Christ and church membership. The object of a church's missions efforts is to meet the needs of persons who are not immediate prospects through self-giving service in the name and spirit of Christ.

Missions is one part of a church's work in fulfilling its total mission or purpose in the world. Missions is the work done by churches in crossing barriers and borders. These barriers may be geographical, racial, cultural, social, physical, or linguistic.

Expressed another way, missions is a church's effort to extend its ministry and witness to persons who are separated from the church by large barriers which must be crossed. These persons live in special circumstances or need. They require specialized approaches to meet their need and to reach them where they are.

Frank K. Means of the Foreign Mission Board reports current writings on missions describe the crossing of borders in terms of the Greek word *oikos* (or "household"). He goes on to say that any fairly distinctive social group, small or large, can constitute some new *oikos* in which the gospel must be proclaimed.

A church's missions responsibility begins in the community where the church is located and extends throughout the world. What a church can do personally in missions work is done through direct action. Direct action is called mission action. What a church cannot do directly, it gets done through representatives.

A church's direct missions work in mission action grows out of the needs which surround a church. The challenge for every church is to decide which needs it will try to meet.

That part of a church's work which it cannot do alone is done in cooperation with other churches through representative agents in the association, state convention, and Southern Baptist Convention.

In representative missions, denominational agencies represent churches in conducting work which a church could not do working alone. Representative missions is action in behalf of churches.

Representative missions work requires support from the churches being represented. This support comes primarily through prayer, finances, and personnel. Adequate support comes only as churches become fully aware of, and assume personal responsibility for, their missions efforts around the world.

Out of a sense of world responsibility each church should perform certain basic missions tasks. These tasks are teach missions, engage in mission action, support world missions through praying and giving, provide and interpret information regarding the work of the church and denomination.

1. Teach Missions

To teach missions means to lead persons to explore with growing understanding the nature and implications of God's missionary purpose and to respond to that purpose in personal commitment and obedience. Awareness and response to God's missionary purpose is a lifelong task for Christians. Throughout the life span church members need to explore the truth about the missions task as set forth in the Bible. They need to discover ways churches fulfil their missions tasks, both in the historical and in the contemporary setting. Church members must prayerfully consider the meaning of God's missionary purpose in today's world. The understandings reached under the leadership of the Holy Spirit must be applied in personal experience as each person assumes responsibility for missions.

To have a meaningful learning experience, persons must be

led to recognize a personal need to learn. Once the missionary imperative of the church is presented, persons need an opportunity to respond through personal commitment.

Curriculum content of missions includes the missionary message of the Bible, the progress of Christian missions, and contemporary missions.

The missionary message of the Bible forms the foundation for missions understandings. Beginning in the Old Testament, man's sin is established as the motivation for God's redemptive missions plan.

The universal love of God finds expression throughout early biblical history. A predominant theme is the divine desire to bring all nations into the knowledge and purpose of this universal love.

The New Testament reveals this divine mission imperative in the coming of Christ and the establishment of the church. Spiritual rebirth through repentance and faith becomes the focus of the mission imperative. The Holy Spirit makes possible the fulfilment of this mission.

As church members experience the meaning and implications of the historical missions plan, they are motivated to face their missions obligation anew.

The study of the progress of Christian missions describes the historical advance of the church in fulfilling its mission. A study of detailed actions from the ascension of Christ to the present reveals the contributions of committed persons to share Christ with others and the value these participants placed upon the mission imperative.

The progress of Christian missions includes the origin, development, and progress of Southern Baptist home and foreign missions under the leadership of the Home Mission Board and the Foreign Mission Board. The emergence of organized state and associational missions programs complements the work of these two boards in fulfilling the church's missions task.

Major emphasis in the teaching task is placed upon contemporary missions. This study includes the current world context in which missions work is done, philosophy of Christian missions, Southern Baptist missions strategy and work, and the missions work of other Christian and non-Christian groups.

To understand missions philosophy and strategy, church members need to know the setting in which missions work is done. World context refers to the geographical, political, cultural, sociological, and economic background of a given area.

The philosophy of Christian missions explores the purpose or motivation for missions. Missions strategy involves the techniques and procedures used in missions work. A study of Baptist missions work involves an examination of what is being done in a given area.

Study of the missions work of other Christian or non-Christian groups helps Baptists see other ways to communicate the gospel of Christ and to evaluate these approaches.

A major emphasis in contemporary missions is placed on church support of representative missions through prayer, finances, and personnel. Tithing is cited as the biblical concept underlying mission support. The church budget, Cooperative Program, and special offerings are channels of the financial support of missions work.

The teaching task is directed to all church constituents, including church members, other persons involved in a church's programs, and their families.

To teach missions, a church must engage in certain essential actions: (a) discover educational needs of persons and select a curriculum plan which meets these needs, (b) provide missions learning opportunities, and (c) enlist persons to study missions.

Certain basic approaches can be used to complete essential actions. To select the appropriate curriculum plan, educational needs must be discovered. Ways include surveys, observation and experience, conferences with church staff and church council, and a review of denominational curriculum plans.

Persons learn about missions through age-level study, churchwide study projects, family study projects, and individual study.

2. Engage in Mission Action

To engage in mission action means to become involved in the church's organized effort to minister and to witness to

persons of special need or circumstance who are not now enrolled or immediate prospects for the church or its programs.

Persons of special need or circumstance will not be reached
unless they are given special attention. The activities of a
church in reaching prospects often miss groups of people who
require not only a witness but also a ministry in Jesus' name.
Mission action combines the elements of ministry and witness
into a missions approach for reaching these people.

Approaches used in mission action in a community are identical to these used in missions work in other parts of the world.

Recipients of mission action include persons in target groups,
and target issues. That action may be preventive, remedial, or
both.

Some of the persons of special need or circumstance are
prisoners, military personnel, alcoholics, and drug abusers, the
poor, language groups, migrants, travelers and tourists, non-
readers, persons in crisis, internationals, the sick, aging, unwed
parents, juvenile delinquents, minority groups, and persons of
nonevangelical faith.

Examples of target issues are social and moral problems
which victimize society.

Correcting these problems is the responsibility of church
members and persons involved in the church's programs and
their families.

To engage in mission action, a church must take three essential actions: (a) discover needs for mission action and select
from those the needs it will meet, (b) provide opportunities
for persons to engage in mission action, and (c) enlist persons
in mission action.

Certain basic approaches are needed to implement essential
actions. Persons may make a survey to discover need. The survey
may occur within the church, reach out to community agencies and institutions, or extend to the association for information
gathered through associational mission action surveys.

Persons can engage in mission action through individual
projects, group projects, unit projects, or churchwide projects.

3. Support World Missions Through Praying and Giving

To support world missions is to promote missions work being

conducted for churches by representative missions programs in the associations, state conventions, and Southern Baptist Convention. These representative programs, commissioned by churches, need the continuing support of churches.

Praying and giving designate the major types of support representative missions programs need. In addition to praying and giving, churches support world missions by creating an environment in which persons can hear and respond to God's call to vocational mission service.

Prayer is the means by which the power of God is brought to bear on the missions task. Intercessory prayer is evidence of one's concern for the lost, oppressed, and hungry everywhere. Every church has a responsibility to help its members become aware of the potential of prayer and to provide opportunities for this experience. The classic example of intercession was in the prayer of Jesus in John 17 as he looked down the course of time and brought the needs of all people before God.

In *The Life of the Church,* Samuel H. Miller describes prayer as a very great thing, larger than a set of words, more than kneeling, but a daring adventure of the spirit engaged in dialogue with God.

A church also has the responsibility for using material resources to extend the gospel to the whole world. The stewardship of material possessions is one of the central teachings of the New Testament. No less a figure than the apostle Paul made it clear that the cause of Christian missions demands support through gifts.

Southern Baptists recognize the tithe as the basic requirement for giving. Special missions offerings represent opportunities for individuals to give beyond the tithe.

The Cooperative Program is the channel of giving for Southern Baptists. Often called the lifeline of missions, the Cooperative Program has been the denomination's plan of financing missions work at home and overseas since 1925. As a Christian tithes through his church, he has a part in all that Southern Baptists are doing.

The church task of supporting world missions is directed toward church members and persons involved in a church's program and their families.

To support world missions, a church must engage in certain essential actions: (a) discover world mission needs which call for church support, (b) provide opportunities for persons to become involved in supporting world missions, and (c) enlist persons to support world missions.

Certain basic approaches can be used to carry out essential actions. World needs which call for church support are found through unit study, mission study groups, churchwide study projects, and individual study and reading.

Opportunities to support world missions through prayer include the use of the prayer calendar by individuals, families, and the congregation; prayer retreats; weeks of prayer for home and foreign missions; and the season of prayer for state missions.

Giving opportunities include the Lottie Moon Christmas Offering, Annie Armstrong Easter Offering, state missions offerings, and the Cooperative Program.

4. Provide and Interpret Information Regarding the Work of the Church and Denomination

Church constituents need to be informed about the work of their church and denomination. All church programs share a common task of communicating this information.

This task means making persons aware of the work of the church and denomination to the point of understanding and motivation for involvement.

This information needs to be vital to the life and work of the church and denomination, relate to the tasks of the missions programs, and respect the age and needs of the recipients.

Leaders of the missions program carry out this task. Members of the program receive the information. Actions essential in performing this task are: (a) secure and receive information from church and denominational sources, and (b) communicate the information to appropriate audiences.

Written communications from association, state, or Southern Baptist Convention programs are used to carry out the essential actions. Included are printed materials a church uses to develop its curriculum plans.

Sources of information are church, state, and Convention-wide meetings; church council and missions program planning groups; and conferences with church staff and other church leaders.

The information is communicated through unit and group meetings.

A CHURCH: IMPLEMENTING ITS MISSIONS PROGRAM

A church implements its missions tasks through the use of church missions program organizations and through organizations beyond the church.

1. Church Missions Program Organizations

The two church program organizations responsible for leading a church in its missions program are Brotherhood for men and boys and Woman's Missionary Union for women, girls, and preschool children.

WMU and Brotherhood perform the same church missions tasks, each in ways appropriate to its constituency. While Woman's Missionary Union and Brotherhood have some distinctive approaches, they also have approaches in common. These common approaches permit joint work by the two organizations in special areas such as churchwide missions projects and mission action.

The work of the two organizations is coordinated in the church council.

Brotherhood and Woman's Missionary Union provide organization and leadership for performing a church's missions tasks. These organizations also provide for men-oriented and women-oriented groupings within a church. These groups deserve consideration as well as the work they do.

Churches need groupings on a church organization level which are distinctively for men and for women. This allows the natural interest of men and of women to find expression in these groupings in a church.

While there are many approaches to learning about missions, supporting missions, and engaging in mission action which are identical for men or women, there are points at which the approach can be made distinctive and thus appeal uniquely to men or women. Some mission action work is best done by women. Other work is best done by men. Some work requires

the joint effort of men and women. In many instances women
have more time to give to missions activities than do men.

In light of all factors, a man's organization and a woman's
organization are suggested as means for a church to use in the
performance of its missions tasks. Brotherhood and Woman's
Missionary Union offer a church organization, leadership, and
innovative approaches for doing missions work.

2. Organization Beyond the Church

Since churches cannot fulfil their world missions responsibility alone, they have created denominational programs and
organizations to represent them in doing some of their work.
Thus churches delegate some of their missions work to such
denominational programs as foreign missions, home missions,
state missions, and associational missions. These programs in turn
are carried out by such organizations as the Foreign Mission
Board, Home Mission Board, state mission board, and associational missions committee.

Denominational missions programs and organizations are
merely an extension of the missions programs of churches.
These programs are agents of the churches, representing them
in places where each church could not go alone. Denominational
missions programs are likewise responsible to the churches they
represent.

Through representative missions for example, a Southern
Baptist church is able to extend its witness to the whole
world through almost 2,500 foreign missionaries serving in
about 70 countries and into all 50 states of the United States
through over 2,000 home missionaries.

Missions organizations in the denomination represent churches
so that churches may express their missions concern on the widest
scale. Churches in turn channel their support of this effort
through prayer, Cooperative Program gifts, special missions offerings, and missions personnel for long- and short-term service.

As denominational missions programs represent churches,
WMU and Brotherhood in the denomination channel information about missions work to the churches through curriculum publications and other materials and keep churches
aware of their role in missions support. WMU and Brother-

hood as denominational agents also assist churches in conducting their direct missions program in the community where
the church is located.

MISSIONS: BREAKING THE MOLD

1. Frontiers in Learning

Many Christians are eager for spiritual man to catch up with
technological man. The statement that the exploration of inner
man must be considered as important as the exploration of outer
space is a cliché by now. Circling the moon, Apollo 8 crew members looked down on the earth, a first which may become common-
place. Frontiers are being extended and barriers are being crossed,
but what of the frontiers in learning?

Some churches are planning learning resource centers which
include films, tapes, recordings, programed books, television sets,
and other audiovisual learning aids.

For instance, a teacher in the church could go to the
resource center, call for the programed tape on the modern
missionary movement, sit at the terminal and begin to see before him paragraphs of information. As he used a light pencil
to trace X on the screen, other information and questions
would appear before him. This programed information would
permit him to progress at his own rate, testing him as he goes.
Wrong answers would flash on the screen with instructions
to call forth other information for review.

Although the programed course may require eight hours,
the teacher could stop at any point, returning as long as six
months later to take up where he left off.

A leader in a youth missions organization may ask technicians
to film his unit meeting on TV tape. At the resource center,
he could view the meeting leisurely to learn what was said and
done. This tape could be stored in the learning resource center
for other leaders in the missions organization to view and use
as part of leader training.

A film on missions work in any country or in any part of the
United States could serve as basic information for a leader who
may test his comprehension later with a programed booklet.

Leader training sessions in a church could be taped and filed
at the resource center for persons who could not attend.

Closed circuit television in a church would make it possible for a single teacher or leader to present basic material at the same time to large groups. Many small groups, meeting all over the church, could then discuss this presentation.

Games of missions strategy may be designed and played by employees of mission boards or even the executive board to determine methods and techniques likely to bring best results in a certain area. War games and academic games now are designed to push up all questions in a mock situation before the actual experience.

Computers could store large amounts of information for church leaders who want to learn faster and more completely than by reading large books.

At Southern Baptist Convention agencies, computers could be programed to translate the Bible into languages and dialects. Rallies and revivals could be televised live to show the United States what is going on in another country or section of the United States.

Southern Baptists may need to consider a computer center where, in seconds, any church could have in hand all the material from all Southern Baptist Convention agencies available to help them work with alcoholics and drug abusers, or any other target group.

Southern Baptists may want to consider investing money in commercial advertisements during televised sports events to reach many nonchurchgoers.

A bright future for astronaut missionaries and bilingual missionaries is assured if Americans establish colonies on the moon, Mars, or other planets to get more living space on earth. These colonies will need missionaries and churches. The possibilities of discovering other life on planets will call for even more missionary activity.

Colonies under the sea will need churches, pastors, and missionaries. Any spiritual ministry needed on earth will be needed above and below earth.

2. Redirected Resources

The time is coming when laser beams will become the lumberjacks of the future and a jungle can be cleared in seconds as a church site; missionaries can fly from Los Angeles to Singapore in thirty-nine minutes at an altitude of 125 nautical miles; picture-phones will enable those calling to see each other; and water guns will reconstitute a whole meal in a small plastic package. When that time arrives, the church will have redirected from necessity its concern and its resources.

We are now dealing with constants. The Holy Spirit is available on request. Money and persons are still needed by churches to devise and to carry out work in the near future. The church, with unlimited power potential, must find itself meeting the financial and personnel demands of the next decade.

Churches will increasingly face the question of priorities in their use of money. Should our churches spend more on self than on others? Will our churches mass property and furnishings while a world waits for food and medicine and the gospel?

Conflicts and resentments between those who have and those who have not will increase. Mobile populations will send Christian families all over the world. Persons who live in a country where they are classified as second-class citizens may provide the empathy needed to help solve some of the problems in this country when they return.

Whatever else the future holds, one of the certainties is people. Many of these persons will have special needs which Christians can meet. Each church must see its community as one aspect of its representative missions work and be ready to share equally its resources in its community, association, and in home and foreign missions areas.

In churches, small groups have a potential for renewal and for using church members in a wide range of ministries.

Brotherhood and Woman's Missionary Union are trying to breathe new life into their traditional programs through small group structure.

In WMU, three approaches to small group work stand out: study groups, prayer groups, mission action groups.

Study groups are oriented toward Bible study, book study, and current missions study. Prayer groups are oriented to intercessory prayer for missions, but they could become prayer sources for church members as well as prayer-sharing opportunities for group members. Mission action groups are oriented to persons of special need.

Brotherhood groups are less formally structured but still

provide a variety of opportunities for men and boys to participate in meaningful mission study, mission action, prayer and giving.

Among the more innovative mission action groups are the headliners and those who seek to rehabilitate prisoners. The headliners group, which concentrates on persons in crisis, follows this process:

Group members write letters of concern of commendation to persons whose situation appears in mass media. Included in each letter is the offer of the church to assist in any way. If the person wants additional assistance, he is asked to call the individual or the church.

A church in Texas has a headliner mission action group which searches the newspaper for people in need. Two persons read the newspaper daily, one searching for needs and the other for persons worthy of commendation.

As the private drama of personal crises unfolds, these persons express their concern in the name of the church and in the name of Christ through telegrams, letters, and other means.

The group concerned with rehabilitating persons to society begins working with the sentenced man before the prison term begins. The group keeps the family together during the period of incarceration and arranges for a job and a second chance in society when the sentence is completed.

The central theme of both groups is: We care. The members of our church care.

What if there were groups like this all over the United States? People would begin to know that Christians care. The sound would at first be strange to some ears, but its strangeness would disappear in the warm response to human hearts hungry for caring.

3. Self-giving Service

In writing about the judgment, Howard Thurman has said that eventually the doer and the deed meet.

> There is a tight circle
> In which man moves.
> Nothing escapes;
> Soon or late,
> Somewhere, somewhen,

> The doer and the deed
> Are face to face! [1]

The sharing-deed and the sharer meet in another person and thus the communion of sharing is begun. The tight circle in which a Christian moves is an encircling love which draws all people in. The first step in sharing is courage. The second is giving self.

More insistently than ever Christians are asking, What can I do? The search for new answers has just begun. In hundreds of churches and in thousands of hearts a response is building.

A church in North Carolina, concerned about sanitation laws in agricultural labor camps, organized a public meeting in a campaign for stronger legislation to improve the condition of migrant camps in the state.

A church in Texas began a day-care center in a Latin American suburb. Doctors gave time, druggists gave medicine, girls rolled bandages, women filled in charts. And the opportunities became more obvious. Some taught English; others, sewing. Men taught other men to drive trucks, use power mowers and hedge clippers, and secure jobs. Women taught other women to run vacuum cleaners, clean house, get their health cards, and secure work as domestics.

A young artist in Georgia began teaching local people to make pottery so they could work—for money.

In Alabama a church began conversational English classes for wives of international students studying at the University Medical Center.

A group of women in a church in a county seat town in South Carolina takes Sunday night supper to the prisoners in the county jail. The men of the church lead a worship service.

A church in Tennessee provides meaningful activities for groups of children after school while these children wait for transportation to their homes.

Some churches in one large city share a social worker who coordinates their work in the inner-city.

Many churches need retired men to help in industrial arts

---

[1] *Inward Journey* (New York: Harper & Row Publishers, 1961).

classes, operate motor pools to take children to therapy, and
teach literacy classes. Retired women are needed to teach, care
for shut-ins, sew and fold bandages, prepare clothes for the
church crisis closet, or take care of a child so another mother
can carry through on her resolve to commit her skills to the
needs of the community.

A church in Pennsylvania opened its chapel every day of
the week and all night. Two hundred visits were recorded
monthly between 7:00 p.m and 2:00 a.m. Now scores of members
meet one night a week to tutor high school youth who are
potential dropouts.

This church opened a teen-age snack shop every Friday
evening and began sponsoring a yearly religious arts festival
where persons try to hear what artists, poets, writers, and musicians of today are saying to the church about God, and about
the church's mission in the world.

In New York a church realized that its changing neighborhood lent itself to some meetings in homes during the week to
study the Scripture passages for Sunday. During one of these
meetings the discussion led to problems of youth and children.
An outgrowth was a youth job night when representatives
of agencies and schools referred youth to jobs.

Discovering that summer library services were not open to
neighborhood children, this church set aside a room in the
church, moved in book shelves, and solicited books and volunteer workers. The library was opened two days a week.

This same church places index cards in the racks and at a
certain time in the service each person writes on a card his
concerns. These concerns are collected and brought to the
Lord's Supper table where the pastor reads them aloud and
builds the morning prayer around them.

In California a church has begun a night ministry. Sixty
volunteers, in teams of two, answer telephone calls from any
person who needs a ministry at night. Other volunteers sit all
night in emergency rooms in case they are needed.

A glimpse of new life in a church may attract those who
have felt the guilt of Christianity when, to them, Christians
have failed to follow Christ without compromise. This same
glimpse may confuse others who have grown up in the institu-

tional church. At the same time, these differences may represent one of the greatest challenges facing Christians today.

What of the future when the cry of the age is show me, don't just talk, show me?

The future calls for persons who will live out in practice all the requirements of a new kind of commitment. That means loving people as they are; serving people where they are; ministering and witnessing to the total man.

Who is the total man?

He is the slum child searching in a cluttered alley, a deaf student who hears volumes with his eyes, the eccentric in the neighborhood boxed in by his loneliness, the lonely apartment dweller, the face that looms out of a crowd.

At the time when commitment is critically necessary, its cost may have risen enormously.

But each Christian in the chaotic seventies must venture past his friendly crowd and the safety of his church building as he seeks to answer for himself, What can *I* do?

The only complete answer is to give his best—himself.

7. The Church in Music Study and
Performance

It happened during the Falls Creek Baptist Assemblies in Oklahoma, and seems to suggest that something unusual is taking place in church music. It would not have seemed so unusual if it had happened only once; but it happened during all four weeks of the assemblies, with different crowds. What happened? Nearly five thousand youth gave an ovation to the choir after the singing of a brief musical composition. They were not applauding the performers; they were evidencing a kind of ecstasy which came as the result of the singing of a sixteenth-century text set to contemporary, "hard-rock" music. Without any attempt to judge the appropriateness of their actions or the spiritual depth of their feelings, one must recognize that some of the generation gap was closed and that communication had taken place. One young man, who came forward accepting Christ during the invitation that followed, said: "If the adult generation cares enough to allow the singing of music that I can understand, then I must give myself to the Christ that prompted such love and concern."

This incident is one of many revealing that today's youth are not satisfied with the status quo—even in the church music they sing and hear. Once again, church music must take on new shape and find new substance. The Now generation is telling us: "Tell it like it is, and when you tell it, speak to us in our own language."

THE EVOLVING PROGRAM

When one considers that the median age is now about twenty-six years and that perhaps a majority of the Church Music program constituency is under the median age, one can begin to see the necessity for new structure and content of the program.

That church music is in the process of change is not particularly new or startling. Church music has been evolving into new patterns and finding new contexts since music was first used in the church. The world continues to change, and church music must be dynamic and relevant to each age.

The transition in the sound, structure, movement, and vocabulary of music is perhaps more obvious today, however, because of the advancement of mass media technology. It is possible now to hear the new sound of music and to hear it almost as soon as it is written. The youth of today have recording devices and receiving sets that were not available a generation ago. Even if a person wished to escape the new sound of music, he can hardly do so.

It seems that the same congregations that so vehemently protested new features in church music a generation ago welcome the innovations of today. All that they require is that the text be appropriate and the theology be sound. Carlton R. Young said: "On the whole, yesterday's congregations and church leaders who were so shocked at the prospect of hearing and participating in these new musical contexts . . . now tend to accept them with a somewhat naive view that the world will, through this music, be brought to the church. This reflects at worst a superficial view of the role of church music, but on the positive side it has made the church aware of the considerable talent in the musical community which has been ignored since the Victorian era." [1]

We continue to hear of the many new forms of church music. Erik Routley, a well-known English hymnologist and

[1] Carlton R. Young, "The Changing Shape of Parish Music," *Church Music*, 67.2, p. 18.

theologian, points out that many of these forms "seem alien to . . . long-standing traditions. There are advocates of jazz, of pop music, of electronic music, of twelve-tone music, and there is no telling what the next suggestion will be." [2] It may be added that, like the chambered nautilus, each new stage of musical development seems to take on added beauty and meaning all its own.

Not all the new forms will make a lasting contribution to church music, but some forms are gradually finding acceptance. Jazz, for instance, is making an impact on church music, and must be considered as a serious and sophisticated musical form. It had its roots in the spirituals of the American Negro. The music of rock-and-roll groups has made inroads into the tastes and performance of the music of American youth. Country and western and gospel forms likewise are popular means of musical expression.

The revival of folk singing in America and other countries has also had its impact on the music of the church. Many people in this country and around the world have been caught up in the ground swell of revolution, dissent, tension, and general protest against existing structures and establishments. Such things are often the substance of the texts of folk music. These new developments are not all bad.

Martin N. Marty said: "Men and women sing new songs when the tradition of the old songs has been spent or when they have something new to sing about." [3] Music is an art that interprets life; thus, we must recognize that folk music will have a bearing on the music that is sung in church. Mr. Marty also states: "The marching music, the song for demonstrations, work songs, protest songs—all are reminiscent of the militant notes sounded by an aggressive church on the move in other ages. The artist or musician who is unmindful of this enlargement of his vocabulary will not be apt to gain a hearing, particularly among the young whose interest in religion will often be non or anti-institutional, anti-establishmentarian, but strongly ethical in outlook." [4] The evolution of church music demands new struc-

2 Erik Routley, *Words, Music, and the Church* (Nashville: Abingdon Press, 1968) , p. 108.
3 Martin N. Marty, "New Patterns for a New Age," *Church Music,* 67.2, p. 1.
4 *Ibid.,* p. 3.

tures, new programs, and new curriculums—all geared to meet the challenge of the new age.

The new forms in chuch music would seem disturbing if it were not also true that in nearly all of church life the movement is "away from tradition, away from academic detachment, and toward personal involvement with the world." [5]

There is new competition today for the minds and souls of people. Riding high on the electronic boom have been the technological advances in television and radio. An unrestrained press has made pornographic literature easily accessible to most persons. In our affluent society, the boat and the sport automobile have become status symbols. Motion picture films for "mature audiences" indicate that we are living in a free and permissive society. The secularist in this kind of environment does not trouble himself about God—he presupposes that God is irrelevant.

Such conditions emphasize that each church program has unlimited opportunities to minister to people in this age. For a program to meet needs, it must go where the action is. We must take advantage of some of the fruits of technological developments. We must train our people in the use of mass communications and present the message through music, art, and literature —expressing the church's concept of love and helping man in his search for life's meaning. We must be zealous activists and innovators as we compete for the souls of men in an increasingly secular society.

THE WORK OF THE NEW MUSIC PROGRAM

What is the work of the music program of a church? Is it important enough to provide resources to insure its success?

The contention is that a Church Music program contributes to the achievement of the church's basic objective of bringing men to Christ and helping them to grow up into Christlikeness. A music program is necessary to meet more fully the physical, emotional, social, and spiritual needs of the individual members. The program provides necessary service in the life and work of a functioning church. Music can be used effectively by a

---

[5] Routley, *op. cit., p.* 43.

properly organized program in providing special ministries in the church and community.

There are many ways of expressing the work of a program. The principal work is best expressed through basic continuing activities or tasks. The new Church Music program is structured to perform four church tasks: Teach music; train persons to lead, sing, and play music; provide music in the church and community; provide and interpret information regarding the work of the church and denomination. These tasks provide the framework for the music program. Work consists not only of the musical service rendered but also of all the musical learning and performance activities in which members engage. *Performance* indicates being and doing for the glory of God rather than showing or exhibiting musical ability for personal glorification.

Through the implementation of the music program tasks, the church offers to its members and prospects opportunities for active participation in musical activities compatible with their backgrounds, needs, and desires.

1. Teaching Music

To teach music means to lead persons to develop musical understandings, attitudes, and perception skills, and also discrimination in music literature and performance. The members of the church are led through appropriate learning activities to study music in order that they may express through music praise to God and witness to God's love. To make the best use of their musical abilities, members need guidance in an exploring study of the content of church music. The major categories of church music content are:

Biblical, historical, and philosophical basis for church music

Music literature—the nature, content, and meaning of the vast heritage of instrumental and vocal church literature

Hymnology—the science of the study of hymnody, including a systematic consideration of origin, development, classification, criticism, and usage

Music theory—the fundamentals of music

Church music history—the story of the development of church music from antiquity to the present time

Elements of music education—music appreciation, rhythmic

response and dramatization, singing, playing of instruments, creating music, and learning to understand musical structure

In order for a church to carry out effectively its task of teaching music, it must engage in certain essential actions:

(1) Discover and analyze music study needs.

(2) Provide appropriate music study opportunities.

(3) Enlist and involve members and prospects in planned musical activities.

There are many approaches to teaching music. Some require organizational structure such as choirs, instrumental groups, music classes, and activity groups. Certain instruction may be given on an individual basis through private lessons or guided home study. Still another means of providing instruction is through programed or self-instruction. Appropriate avenues of instruction to the congregation as a whole include such activities as recitals, concerts, hymn sings, hymn rehearsals, and seasonal musical presentations.

Particular attention is given in the study of music to meeting the developmental and maturational needs of the members. Appropriate musical activities should be provided for all ages on the basis of each learner's readiness to engage in a particular activity. The emphasis should be on leading persons to grow toward spiritual maturity through involvement in church music, as well as to grow in their understanding of musical experiences and to develop specific musical abilities.

2. Training Persons to Lead, Sing, and Play Music

To *train* means to guide persons in learning experiences designed to develop their performing abilities. Teaching emphasizes *knowing*; training emphasizes *doing*.

Music education includes both teaching and training. Training, although including many elements of teaching, is related more to the educational process designed to improve personal and group performance. Specifically, musical training is concerned with the development of motor skills of leaders and members in order that they may become skilful in the act and art of leading, singing, or playing music.

Three categories of musical training are provided through the Church Music program: skill training, training for specific positions, and training in the use of leadership methods and materials. Music leaders and members look to the training program of their church for any general training needed, since it is responsible for providing this type of training. Specialized musical training is the responsibility of the Church Music program because it is uniquely equipped to develop and utilize the musical skills of the church constituency. All training that is provided in the church is coordinated through the church council.

Basic avenues for providing musical training to leaders and members of the church are the rehearsals of vocal and instrumental groups; rehearsals of the congregation as a whole; lessons for individual vocalists and instrumentalists; classes for vocalists, instrumentalists, and leaders; and individual home study.

In providing training, the Church Music program should lead members to become increasingly aware of the need of using God-given musical talents and developing the mental and motor skills necessary for successful musical participation and performance in the church and community. The church, through a well-planned program of musical training, can hope to have a sufficient number of persons who are able to lead, play, and sing accurately, skilfully, artistically, and expressively.

3. Providing Music in the Church and Community

The music program will supply the church with the organization and leaders for the music needs of the church. *Music,* as it is used here, means music literature such as hymns, anthems, and instrumental and vocal works; music supplies and equipment such as educational devices, instruments, and curriculum materials; and musical service in the various areas of church life. In essence, the Church Music program will be responsible for the music of the congregational services; assist the other church program organizations with their music as requested; provide counsel, guidance, and musical services to the church members at weddings, funerals, and other occasions as requested; provide counsel and guidance relative to music in the home and to music as a church vocation; and initiate and conduct musical witnessing projects in the church and community.

A study of the New Testament bears witness to the generally recognized concept that the church is a fellowship of baptized believers making up the body of Christ and that this body—living and vital—has certain characteristic expressions or activities that are natural and vital to its being. These functions that help sustain the body may be identified as worship, witness, educate, minister, and apply. Only as the music program gives expression to the performance of these five functions can it fulfil its purpose.

The primary focus of the task is on the development and utilization of the musical talents of the church constituency in the church, home, and community. To realize this outcome, the church must take certain essential actions, such as: (1) discover musical performance and service opportunities; (2) provide performance and service activities; (3) enlist persons in performance and service activities; (4) involve persons in musical performance and service experiences; (5) provide musical assistance to individuals, families, and church program organizations; (6) and lead members to express the church's functions through musical activities.

The opportunities for performing the functions of worship, witness, educate, minister, and apply God-given talent in daily living are almost limitless. The most obvious service opportunity is the regular congregational services on Sunday, in midweek, and in special services such as revivals. Assisting with the music in church-type missions and chapels is another opportunity. The music program also feels responsible for assisting with the music in other church program organization meetings, in Vacation Bible Schools, and at church camps, retreats, assemblies, and conferences. Unique indeed is the opportunity of the music program to assist in the congregational services that are broadcast or televised, and occasionally to present special musical programs via radio and television.

The music program can cooperate with the missions program of the church in many ways. Numerous churches are encouraging their choirs to participate in special witnessing projects throughout their community and in other cities and states. Some groups are assisting Vacation Bible Schools, mission music programs, and music schools. Others are performing special ministries through music in institutions, for the homebound, and for other persons with special needs.

Most of these suggestions are group-oriented approaches.

Equally important are the opportunities for using God-given musical talents on an individual basis. Churches should encourage the use of individual talents in leading, singing, or playing music, particularly in community affairs where a Christian witness is needed. Churches should be actively engaged in calling out its members and training and encouraging them to use their special gifts as effectively as possible in the spreading of the gospel.

4. Providing and Interpreting Information Regarding the Work of the Church and Denomination

Church members need to know what the church and the denomination are doing. All church program organizations share the responsibility for providing information about the work of the various denominational agencies.

To *provide* means that the Church Music program (among others) will be responsible for procuring and supplying information. To *interpret* suggests that the music program will explain information or represent it by audio or visual means. *Information* includes news, materials, programs, and knowledge —all of which may be derived from reading, observation, instruction, or personal communication.

The information provided should be vital to the life and work of the church and the denomination, compatible with music program tasks, and in keeping with the age, maturity, and needs of the recipients. This information, collected from many sources, may be shared through spoken, sung, or written communication. It should be provided in time to relate properly to the individual or group and in time for the action to be carried out on schedule. The information is shared not only in the church and in the home but through personal communications according to the nature of the material.

It is important that Southern Baptist churches work together toward worthy objectives. Coordination and cooperation are possible only when the lines of communication are kept open between church members and denominational leaders.

DESIRED OUTCOMES THROUGH THE NEW PROGRAM

Do you teach music or do you teach people? This age-old

question has been the topic of many discussions among musicians. It is not an easy question to answer. Those who are primarily concerned with music education would answer that you teach people. Those whose leanings are toward musical performance would say that you teach music. Some would say that you cannot take one position over against the other.

To state the question another way, should the Church Music program place primary attention on what the leaders and members can do for the church or should primary attention be given to what the church can do for its leaders and members? Stated yet another way, should the music program give primary attention to music education, with musical performance being the outgrowth of music education experiences or should the music program exist primarily for musical performance, with music education included in the curriculum to improve musical performance?

Neither of the above positions seems adequate. There must be a balance between study and action. To emphasize either direction to the neglect of the other is not best. In *Journey Inward, Journey Outward*,[6] the author described the experiences of her church in trying to hold the proper balance between the structures that allow people to be on the "inward journey" and those that would get people involved with the world's need. The Church Music program of the seventies is geared to take both the "inward journey" and the "outward journey." These journeys are expressed here in terms of encounters. They represent the dimensions of a fully developed program and should be considered as three parts of a whole—each dependent on the other.

1. Encounter with Self

The encounter with self is needed for the individual to discover his inner being. "Who am I? Why do I exist? Do I have special gifts that God can use?" These are some of the basic questions each person will be led to face. To know God fully, one must know himself. The music program will seek to help persons find worth within themselves—worth because they are created by God.

---

[6] Elizabeth O'Conner, *Journey Inward, Journey Outward* (New York: Harper & Row, Publishers, 1968).

2. Encounter with God

An individual never succeeds in knowing himself until he seeks to know God. One needs to realize that a requirement for encounter with God is a "turning of body and spirit to God." We teach music so that people can better experience the presence of God and realize more fully his indescribable mysteries. Through musical experiences we point the way to Christ, for Christ is the way men know God. This dimension is eternal. Finding worth in God is a countinuing adventure for Christians.

Worship is encounter with one of worth—God, explains J. P. Allen.[7] Worship is to respond to God and in that context to understand oneself. Through worship, a true dimension of life can come into focus. If we know God, who he is, and who we are, we should take time frequently for spiritual refreshment through individual and corporate worship.

As a program, Church Music has impressive responsibilities for guiding the encounter of the congregation through spiritual musical experiences. This is the encounter when Christians bring themselves, their talents, and their gifts and present them in a joint offering to God.

Encounter suggests involvement. Music involves the congregation in praise, adoration, intercession, confession, repentance, testimony, and commitment of life as they experience a vital relationship with God. The music program, perhaps as no other program, must emphasize the necessity of encounter between God and his people.

3. Encounter with Others

Music is a medium for understanding other people, their culture, their problems, their joys, their frustrations, their happiness, their bewilderment, their ecstasies, and their disillusionment. Through encounter in the community, music program members can be led to see reality in human life. They can be led to become heralds of glad tidings, messengers of peace.

Music is a means of communication. It is a channel for the transfer of the experiences of people in terms of sound and

---

[7] J. P. Allen, *Reality in Worship* (Nashville; Convention Press, 1965).

emotion. As a language, music has the power to stimulate feelings, to arouse emotions, to shape attitudes, and to influence the thoughts and concepts of people. As some have expressed it, music is a means of spiritual impression and spiritual expression. It may be used to express one's own feelings, but at the same time be a powerful instrument to arouse feelings in the hearts of the listeners.

The unequalled power of music to sway the thoughts and emotions of people has long been recognized. The new Church Music program will capitalize on this power in its activities to proclaim the gospel through choral and instrumental music in the church and community. It will be used as a means of declaring the good news that God has provided redemption from sin. Illustration after illustration can be given describing the activities of churches in sending their organized musical groups to share the gospel in places where the gospel has not been proclaimed.

Recently, a choir from a Southern state accepted an invitation to participate in an evangelistic crusade in a Northern metropolitan area. The choir members spent months in preparation. They studied the arts of visitation, personal witness, and biblical interpretation. They practiced singing music suited to the needs of the project. During the crusade, they visited hundreds of homes during the day and sang at the services in the evening. Scores of people made commitments to Christ. After returning home the choir became a more dynamic force for outreach in their church. Many of the choir members committed their lives to church vocations.

It has been reported by hundreds of church choirs as they have toured the nation that getting a hearing is never difficult. People of all races and creeds have stopped and listened as the choir members expressed the love that they have for Christ. The response to a sharing of personal testimonies through music has been overwhelming and gratifying.

It is said that the greatest opportunity for communicating the gospel in the seventies will be through art, drama, and music. Christians have amazingly good news to tell. They are able to express to the world that they have confidence in Christ as Saviour and Lord and in the verity of God's love.

The Church Music program will be structured as never before to reach out into the community and feel the heartbeat of people and to utilize the gifts of all its members in vital, relevant, Christian service.

These encounters describe the desired results of the new music program. In the encounters there must be a balance betwen musical performance and the renewing experiences in the internal church activities. One cannot encounter people in their unconcerned condition in the supermarkets, the coffee houses, the shopping malls, or mission stations without sensing the need for renewal that comes from encounter with God. Through the renewing of the inner life, members will find self-satisfaction, self-fulfilment, and reason for self-giving. Music will help people discover the true meaning of the abundant life.

8. *Training for a Dynamic Church*

Change is inevitable. It always has been. In the past, however, changes occurred much more slowly than they do today. Then, knowledge was gained more slowly, and news was communicated less rapidly.

Now the knowledge explosion has speeded up the rate of change. The world's accumulated knowledge doubles every few years. Changes occur swiftly. People hardly have time to adjust to something new before something newer replaces it.

To function effectively in today's world, persons and organizations must be geared to change.

THE CHALLENGE OF CHANGE

A church cannot stand still. It must keep up or slip back. Changes in the world affect the life and work of the church. The church needs members trained to meet creatively today's challenge of change.

Projections about life in the seventies foresee considerable upheaval in the value systems of our society.[1] Honesty in business, sex behavior, the role of the home and parents, race relations,

---

[1] Information about life in the 70's is based on material in "Report of Work Group IV, SBC '70 Onward Planning," an Inter-Agency Council Report, July, 1966, pp. 36–44.

and labor-management problems are only a few of the areas in which standards are shifting. These changing patterns call for church members trained to meet the challenge of applying Christian principles in perplexing situations.

Family life will face greater tests in the seventies because there will be more working mothers, more neglected children, increasing unfaithfulness, unemployment, and juvenile delinquency. These pressures on family life call for church members trained to maintain strong Christian families.

Changes in occupations call for churches trained to adjust schedules and activities to meet the challenge posed by new types of jobs, unusual working hours, and increasing leisure time.

Changes in education call for church leaders trained to provide educational opportunities that are equal to, or better than, those provided outside the church.

The generation gap—wider now than ever—calls for leaders trained to communicate the unchanging truths of the Christian faith to a generation more willing to accept the changing than the changeless. Even though adults may find change difficult to accept, youth not only accept but expect it. For many the status quo is to be questioned, not preserved. Sharp, inquiring minds are probing more deeply into the reasons for commonly accepted beliefs, customs, and standards of morality.

Church members have always needed training, but never before has the challenge to train been so great. Trained, committed church members are needed to communicate the gospel to today's world.

A NEW SPIRIT AND A NEW NAME IN TRAINING

The mood of the age is a quest for something better than life as it has been. The search for meaning in life and for vitality in religion is intense. Increasing numbers who need the gospel look upon Christians with growing disillusionment and suspicion. They see the church as willing to talk about love and concern, but too self-centered, uninformed, or inept to do more than talk.

If churches are to fulfil their mission in this age, leaders and members must be trained. A new attitude toward training as well as a deeper commitment to training in a church must be instilled in the hearts of church leaders and other church members.

During the last four decades most Southern Baptist churches have provided general church membership training for all church members and basic religious instruction for young children. In recent years some churches have also provided an orientation class for new church members. Leadership training for workers in the training program and for general officers and committees has been provided in many churches.

In studying the nature and functions of a church and identifying all work which a church should carry on, the following tasks have been stated as making up the training program of a church:

(1) Orient new church members.

(2) Train church members to perform the functions of the church.

(3) Train church leaders.

(4) Teach Christian theology, Christian ethics, Christian history, and church polity and organization.

(5) Provide and interpret information regarding the work of the church and denomination.

This statement of tasks clarifies and sharpens areas of work which have been a part of a church's training program in the past. It also broadens the responsibilities of a training program, especially in the areas of new church member orientation and church leader training, to include activities which have not been generally identified with the training program as it has been expressed through the Training Union organization.

As new understandings of the church training program have developed, many Southern Baptists have felt that a new name for the program might help communicate the new and larger role training should have in the churches.

An intensive search was made for a new name that would be brief, memorable, descriptive, appealing, and yet would build on the best from the past. The process of selecting the name involved hours of discussions, correspondence, study, and prayer in which many persons and groups in Baptist life participated. The name selected was QUEST.

The new name reflects man's search for meaning, the Christian's desire for continuing growth in understanding and service, the need of the church to find new and better ways to share unchanging truth in a rapidly changing world.

QUEST could not exist apart from the church. It has no reason for being except to meet the training needs of a church and of church members. It works with individuals as church members, helping them develop so that they may function effectively as members of the body of Christ. It is a QUEST for commitment to the life and work of a church, a QUEST for involvement in the life and work of a church, and a QUEST for effectiveness in fulfilling the mission of a church.

The training program relates to all other church programs and services. It supports each by:

(1) Helping new church members understand and participate appropriately in opportunities for growth and service provided by church programs and services.

(2) Helping church members develop skills that will enable them to participate effectively in fulfilling a church's mission through other programs and services.

(3) Helping all church members to discover their potential for service in church-elected positions, and guiding their preparation and training in order that they become more fruitful and effective. QUEST will serve as the training ground of workers and leaders for every endeavor of a church.

The training program attains its goals when church members are trained to work together within the fellowship of a church and to be effective members of Christ's body wherever they are. It succeeds when the church is worshiping, witnessing, educating, ministering, and applying the gospel with growing power and effect. It succeeds when individuals give evidence of being responsible members of a dynamic church in laboring together, empowered by the Spirit, to bring men to God through Christ.

QUEST FOR COMMITMENT—NEW CHURCH MEMBER ORIENTATION

Many churches carry on their rolls countless members who are only nominally committed to Christ and the church. Without genuine conversion there can be no Christian commitment. Conversion and commitment are basic if one is to be Christ-centered in his motivation and involvement in the life and work of a church in the world. Churches with relatively few committed members will not be the dynamic churches required by the challenges of the seventies.

If this weakness in church life is to be remedied, persons being received into church membership need to be sure of their conversion. They need to become informed, committed participants in the life and work of a church. This is true of both new Christians and transfer members. The training program task "orient new church members" is designed to help them achieve this commitment.

"To orient" means to acquaint with a situation, to set in the right direction, to put into correct relationship. In orienting new church members, a church shows its love and concern for them. Through new member orientation a church may tie together more effectively its evangelistic and educational efforts. The new church member receives appropriate help as he progresses toward Christian maturity and effectiveness.

1. Providing Orientation

To implement the task "orient new church members," a church needs to carry out certain essential actions.

First, all persons being received into the church should be enlisted to participate in the orientation provided. As a step toward accomplishing this, some churches find it helpful to adopt a policy concerning the participation of new members in orientation. Such a policy is evidence of a church's commitment to adequate orientation for all new members. After a person has presented himself for church membership, follow-up visits may help him become involved in orientation. Visits may be made by the pastor or other church staff members, deacons, and other church leaders, including new member orientation personnel.

Special events scheduled at regular intervals help new members feel the church's welcome and concern. A banquet, fellowship, or reception may be held for this purpose.

An adequate orientation program will also provide opportunities for both the church and the new member to verify their relationship and commitment to each other. Too much emphasis cannot be placed on the importance of a regenerate church membership. Emphasis may be given through sermons, special studies, counseling, or a church's articles of faith.

Counseling sessions for new members will help each one re-affirm his conversion and his commitment to Christ and the church. These sessions will also help the new member understand the church's commitment to him.

Each new member needs opportunities to express through testimony his understandings and feelings regarding his conversion experience. Parents of young converts may need training in understanding their child's experience and in guiding his spiritual development.

Through new church member orientation a church can provide experiences to deepen the new member's understanding and commitment. This can be accomplished through a series of instruction sessions dealing with the church and its covenant, its beliefs, its history, and its program and organization. Instruction for new converts will need to give more attention to the nature of the Christian life and the implications of Christian faith for daily living. Such instruction sessions are more effective when the teaching can be tailored to meet the needs of the new members. For example, older children who join the church need to be separated from adult new members during this instruction so that the instructor will be able to meet more effectively the need of both.

Effective new church member orientation should help lead the new member to become involved in the life and work of a church. There are many ways to accomplish this. Some churches place great stress upon getting new members involved in the church program organizations designed to meet their needs. Others use special activities such as fellowships, banquets, and recognition services to call attention to the need for continued involvement. Some churches have found it wise to assign faithful church members as sponsors to give oversight to new church members. The sponsor may be an individual or a family. In either instance, the purpose is to help, guide, counsel, and encourage the new member to find his place in the church's life.

A church will likely find it wise and helpful to review periodically how well new members have become actively involved in the life of the church. This practice will help a church know when action is needed to prevent a new member from joining the ranks of the inactive.

2. The Benefits of Orienting New Church Members

The basic benefit to be derived from accomplishing this task is the commitment of church members to Jesus Christ as Saviour and Lord and to participation in the work of the church. When new church members make this commitment, they can be led to participate in other types of training. They can be led more easily to take part in other church programs and services so as to enrich their lives and contribute to the effectiveness of the whole church. Gradually, the church will find that more of the members are helping to fulfil the church's mission. A greater spirit of commitment and fellowship will grow within the church. Every new member and the church will know and understand what each expects of the other in the covenant relationship.

QUEST FOR INVOLVEMENT

The New Testament teaches that all church members are to have a part in fulfilling the mission of the church. The need for these members to be trained for effective service grows out of the nature, purpose, and functions of a church. The church is the body of Christ, created to do his work in the world. Every member is to be a functioning part of the body, devoted to carrying out the will of Christ, the head. Each member must develop the capabilities needed, just as a growing child must develop the understandings and skills required to meet the demands of each stage in life.

More than ever before, the gospel must be demonstrated daily in the lives of Christians if it is to be effectively communicated to modern man. Many Christian leaders believe that one of the deepest needs and greatest opportunities of Christian work today is the faithful, day-to-day worship, witness, learning, and ministry by each church member as he applies the gospel in his daily activities. However, a study of most Baptist churches will reveal that a relatively small percentage of the members are involved in carrying on the work of the church in either individual or group activities. More members need to share in the work. Effective Christian service requires training in skills. Beyond orientation, every church should provide training which will equip the members for involvement in the church's mission.

Two tasks of the training program are designed to equip church members for Christian service. The first is train church members to perform the functions of the church. The second is teach Christian theology, Christian ethics, Christian history, and church polity and organization.

Training has been described as an educational process designed to improve individual and group performance. Considering training more from the viewpoint of the learner, LeRoy Ford of Southwestern Seminary defines it as "the process of acquiring the learnings (understandings, attitudes, knowledge, skills), essential to the skilful, efficient performance of assigned responsibilities." [2] Both of these definitions place the emphasis on learning to do—to become involved in fulfilling the church's mission.

Training church members to perform the functions of the church means helping them acquire the learnings and self-discipline they need as responsible, committed church members. While this task emphasizes the development of skills, it also assumes a solid foundation of necessary knowledge, understandings, and attitudes on the part of the member. This foundation is provided through the curriculum areas of the second member training task, as well as through the study of curriculum areas of other church program organizations.

The study of Christian theology will help church members deepen their understanding of biblical teachings and organize their beliefs into a personal theology. A church member who has developed his own system of valid beliefs about God and his relation to man will be better able to reflect his beliefs in personal attitudes and daily actions.

Christian ethics is concerned with God's ideals for living. These ideals are set forth in the Scriptures and thus provide the "oughtness" of the Christian life. A study of Christian ethics is intended to help persons grow in Christian character and the ability to express and apply it in every relationship of daily living. The scope of Christian ethics is as broad as life itself. The faith that brings salvation is to be lived in obedience to the God who saves. Every issue of life needs the application of the gospel.

---

2 LeRoy Ford, *Developing Skills for Church Leaders* (Nashville: Convention Press, 1968), p. 12.

Christian history is concerned with the record of God's dealings with men, as he prepared for and gave the revelation of himself in Christ. It includes the biblical witness to the origin and early development of the church. It reveals the moral and ethical triumphs and defeats of the Christian church as a part of all that God has done in and through the Christian movement. Studies in this area help persons to discover and benefit from meaning and values in Christian history.

Church polity and organization concerns the form of government and organizational framework through which Baptist churches work. A study of church polity and organization can help persons know how and why a Baptist church does its work. Knowing this, persons are more likely to be motivated to involve themselves intelligently and actively in the work.

1. Providing Church Member Training

In order to train its members, a church must analyze training needs periodically. Those responsible for planning member training must consider the question, What training is needed? A thorough survey should be made to determine general training needs and interests of church members. A church which is deeply interested in meeting the training needs of its members could do a formal survey of the membership by mail and through church meetings. The members could be given opportunity to indicate types of training in which they are interested and times when it would be convenient to meet with a group for the study (or to use individual training materials).

In addition to what may be learned through a survey, leaders of the training program can study the goals or projects planned by the church and determine the training needed to attain the goals or carry out the projects. For instance, if the church is planning a strong effort to visit and reclaim inactive members, training in doing this kind of visitation could be offered through the training program at the most advantageous time.

Within the training groups, persons already enrolled can be given opportunity through the regular planning sessions of their group to have a part in selecting training units which will meet their needs for the period being planned. Conversations with members of these groups and with other church members may reveal to leaders of the training program other training needs to be met.

Another way to determine training needs is by identifying "advance groups." These are specific individuals (usually not involved in the training program) who because of their needs or interests may be ready for a particular kind of training. For example, parents of elementary-age children might respond to a study of how children learn. Senior Adults who can attend training sessions at a time other than Sunday night might be such a group. Another group might include Adults who attend Wednesday night church supper and prayer meeting but have no responsibility during officers and teachers' meetings. A significant number of persons might have training needs which could be met at this time.

When a church has a clear picture of the training needs of the members, the next step is to provide opportunities for the training. The majority of the training will be offered through training groups. These may be ongoing groups and short-term groups.

Most church member training is accomplished in continuing groups formed on an age-graded basis. However, some church members respond to training which runs for a specified time period and is planned to accomplish a specific purpose. Experience has shown that some Adults prefer not to be enlisted "for life" in a continuing training group. Short-term training groups are suggested as an approach for reaching such adults for training. But short-term training should not be conducted at the expense of the ongoing training of Adults.

Most training groups will meet on Sunday evenings, but a church should plan to make training available at times which are convenient to the group involved. For example, mothers of school-age children could attend training sessions on weekdays. Persons who serve in the training program might want additional training on a Sunday afternoon, week night, or Saturday. Though Sunday evening may be the prime time in most churches, a church will do well to think in terms of schedules flexible enough to meet training needs discovered.

In addition to training which may be offered through group experience, a church will do well to make attractive and appealing individual study materials available to members. The church library may be the means of collecting, storing, and circulating these materials to members. An increasing number of training materials will include programed instruction, workbooks, individual study guides, and audiovisual helps. Record sets or tapes which teach principles of basic subjects such as learning or witnessing will become more common. An advantage of training materials designed for individual use is that they enable the learner to make his own schedule and use bits of time which might otherwise be wasted. This will become increasingly important as life becomes more complex. The advance of technology may soon make it practical for some churches to make training activities available in the homes of members through the use of home televisions or telephone attachments, supplemented with printed materials.

Another training approach is to suggest guided reading programs in areas of interest. Books for these programs can be made available to the membership through the church library. For example, a young Adult who is rethinking his personal theology may need a carefully planned reading program in Christian theology. Couples who are expecting their first child could benefit from a reading program about skills needed in providing a healthy Christian home for the expected child.

Other training can be offered through camps, retreats, conferences, or projects emphasizing one or more skill areas. A church might sponsor a brief conference or retreat designed to help families improve their skills in family worship. A similar approach could be used in preparing the church membership for participating in an evangelistic effort by the church.

In addition to these activities, a church should plan to offer advanced training and depth studies to those who are ready for them.

Though much of the training in groups will be done at the church, the formation of neighborhood groups meeting in home, downtown luncheon groups, on-campus groups in college towns, and the like should not be overlooked as a means of providing training.

Training to develop skills may include practice in applying the skills being developed. Whenever possible, the opportunities for practice should be provided through participation in activities being carried on by other church programs and services. When this is not practical, the QUEST training group will provide opportunities for practice and evaluation in connection with the training unit.

At times, specific training may be offered to help church members become meaningfully involved in a special project of a church program. For example, training needed by church members to carry out a special emphasis on outreach through the Sunday School could be offered through QUEST. Some training opportunities may be designed specifically for youth.

Though a church may analyze training needs and provide a variety of training opportunities, it still faces the challenge of involving the membership in the training provided. This will be easier when training opportunities have been planned to meet the expressed needs of members. However, it will still be necessary in most churches to challenge the membership to respond to a biblical concept of the place of training in a Christian's life. A strong emphasis from the pulpit will help. A well-planned campaign of communication and promotion through bulletins, church papers, special mailings, and special studies will reach some. Others can be reached by a personal appeal through visitation, phone calls, or letters. The appeal of a flexible schedule will reach still others.

Improving the quality and appeal of training offered may reach and challenge some members. The cooperative and supportive efforts of leaders of other church programs and services are helpful in enlisting church members in QUEST. Social gatherings also help to involve persons.

A church which believes in the imperative of training will go all-out to involve the members in training which will equip them to function as responsive members of Christ's body, the church.

As members are trained, a church should guide them to find opportunities to apply the knowledge, understandings, and skills they are gaining. During training units and after their completion, training program leaders should encourage members to become involved in specific service opportunities available through church programs and services. Leaders of other church programs and services should help QUEST leaders in their efforts to lead members to use their training in the outreach, witnessing, ministering activities being carried on by the church.

In addition to the training provided for church members a church can also provide for the needs of Preschoolers and Children in connection with these two tasks. Age-graded departments for these divisions can offer foundational training experiences to acquaint the children with the functions of the church and develop appropriate understandings of Christian theology, Christian ethics, and church polity and organization. For Preschoolers the training program and other church programs share a unified curriculum.

2. The Benefits of Church Member Training

When church members participate in appropriate training opportunities, many benefits are realized by them individually and by the church as a group. Individual and church training needs will be met.

As persons come to grips with the subject areas upon which member training opportunities are built, they are "rooted and built up in him [Christ], and established in the faith" (Col. 2:7). Out of such training church members can develop sound beliefs and Christian standards of conduct. Since becoming a Christian does not remove a person from the world of reality, help and guidance in practical application of Christian truth must be continually available. This can be offered through QUEST.

Church members in any generation need to be made aware of the contributions made to Baptist life by Christian heroes of the past. Baptists have a great and colorful history. It is a story of dedication which overcame ridicule and persecution. It is a record of deep faith and profound conviction. The work of today and tomorrow can best be accomplished when church members appreciate the heritage upon which much of the present program is based. The training program provides both the setting and the subject matter for enabling church members to develop such an appreciation.

By comparison, more splits within church fellowship come about over differences of practice and procedure than over differences of doctrinal position. The way a church makes its decisions and does its work is a needed subject for discussion. In QUEST, church members gain an acquaintance with Baptist polity and organization. This can result in broader and more active participation in decisions which the church must make about its practices and procedures.

Undergirded by knowledge and understanding gained through study of curriculum areas included in member training, persons need to be equipped to "observe [do, perform] all things which I [Christ] have commanded" (Matt. 28:20). A person needs adequate and well-developed Christian skills to express his beliefs in words and actions.

When the two church member training tasks are carried on together, the "equipping of the saints for the work of service" (Eph. 4:12, NASB)[3] becomes a reality. The trained church member will know the gospel and will know how to share it in compassionate witness and ministry. He will contribute to the total life of the church as he takes seriously the words of Jesus, "If ye know these things, happy are ye if ye do them" (John 13:17).

QUEST FOR EFFECTIVENESS

Every church needs dedicated, trained leaders to help guide members to achieve the church's goals. What church has enough qualified leaders for its programs? What church does not face these problems:

—vacant places of leadership
—many overworked leaders carrying multiple jobs
—a rapid turnover of leaders
—an increasing number of unreached persons

Too many adult church members are either indifferent spectators or spiritual infants unable to serve the Lord as mature Christians. Because many church members have not been developed for service by their churches, more leadership responsibility is heaped upon the sagging shoulders of a few. For too long a faithful few have been called on to do the work of many. These leaders need to be relieved of some of their responsibilities in order that they may perform effectively and with growing satisfaction in the jobs they do accept. In addition, many leaders need additional training for their jobs, but their burden

---

[3] *New American Standard Bible: New Testament,* © The Lockman Foundation, 1960, 1962, 1963.

of multiple responsibilities allows neither time nor energy for improvement. Other leaders should be trained to take over some of the responsibilities carried by these overworked leaders.

These problems point to the urgent need for an organized effort to discover and develop for service those members who have from God the gifts needed by leaders. Providing training for leaders grows out of the biblical concept of volunteer leadership in a church. This concept is consistent with Christ's call to discipleship.

The task of training church leaders includes training for any church-elected leadership responsibility commonly held by lay members of a church. The training is designed to help the trainee develop increased competence to serve effectively and efficiently.

Training is more than knowledge. It is a process. It includes attitudes, understandings, and skills. The influence of the instructor may be greater than that of the content of the course. Much leader training is caught rather than taught. The desired attitudes and understandings come through association with a dedicated instructor, the trials of learning, the discovery of worthy goals, and the joys of accomplishment.

The leader training task provides opportunity for each member and leader to discover and develop his potential for service. He is helped to understand where he is likely to be most effective as a leader. In addition to providing basic preparation for service, church leader training offers continuing opportunities for growth and development on the job.

Many persons assume leadership responsibility without training. In fairness to them and to those they lead, it is a church's duty to help them learn how to serve well. The requirements of a leader in service are different from those of a potential leader. The leader in service will require more specific and immediate help with job skills and knowledge of his work. At first, he will likely want to concentrate on training which aids him in immediate performance. Later he will see a need for deeper study, development of broader or more advanced skills, or activities designed to improve his attitudes and motivations in service.

These leader training needs have led to the identification of specific subject areas in which materials are being prepared to help churches train their leaders. Under the heading "General Leadership Training" are:

• *Introductory Courses in Church Leadership.*—Materials dealing with a basic understanding of a church and its history, a survey of leadership skills, understanding the Bible, Baptist doctrines, and other suitable subjects will be included in this area.

• *Understanding Age Levels and Special Groups in a Church.*—This area includes materials on age-group characteristics and methods, including work with Preschoolers, Children, Youth, and Adults. It also includes materials on work with special groups, such as the mentally retarded, the gifted, and others.

• *Developing General Leadership Skills.*—This area includes training in skills needed by leaders in several programs and services of a church. Materials will deal with such subjects as principles of effective planning, principles of group dynamics, skills in communication, and principles of leading effective learning.

The training program will have primary responsibility for offering training in these three subject areas.

The second grouping is "Specialized Leadership Training." It includes the administration of church programs and services and deals with concepts, job duties, and job skills needed in the programs or services. Specialized leadership training is the responsibility of the program or service concerned. A program or service may request the training program to provide or assist with training in these subject areas.

Within a program much on-the-job training is done through practice and consultation with leaders who are immediately available to provide technical or specialized training.

1. Providing Church Leader Training

Training church leaders is no easy task. It requires a church to analyze and determine its leadership needs. Any plan for determining leader training needs in a church should insure that the needs of all phases of a church program are reflected. Plans may include such activities as personal consultation between the chief officers of the various church organizations, an analysis of existing leadership vacancies, and a study of the anticipated turnover of leadership at the beginning of a church year.

Another step in providing leader training is to identify and schedule the types of training needed. Either general or specialized training may be taken before one begins to serve or while he is serving.

Preservice training is for persons who have never held a church-elected place of service, have not recently held a place of service, or are preparing to accept a different type of leadership responsibility. This training should include counseling or self-evaluation tools which will assist the trainee in developing an adequate training plan in keeping with personal goals and church leadership needs. The need for leaders may force judgments as to what training is essential to meet the minimum standards of service. For example, the pressing need for a group of leaders to staff the vacancies in work with Adults could suggest that a preservice course in the "Art of Group Leadership" be offered. It could be followed with personal conferences in specific procedures related to the job and in the use of materials available for leaders. This plan might be followed with specific training as in-service training soon after the leaders have begun to serve.

In-service training is for persons holding church-elected positions. This training assists leaders in determining their training needs and in securing appropriate training. It is a means of providing additional training as needed to enable persons to function more effectively in their present places of service. It may include any or all of the Christian leadership subject areas discussed earlier.

Some training may deal with developing skills needed in more than one church program or service. For example, training in the skill of communication or in the skill of group leadership may be offered by training program leaders for persons representing several organizations.

Much of the leadership training for which QUEST is responsible may be scheduled on Sunday during the regular time when other QUEST groups are meeting. Additional sessions may be scheduled at other times to meet needs and avoid conflict with assigned duties.

Each church needs to discover and recruit persons to participate in training. Every Adult church member is a potential leader. Potential leaders may also be found among older members of the Youth division. Many church members need help and encouragement in discovering and developing their leadership potential. Many Christians are not so much limited by their past as by their lack of vision of their future in Christ. They must be taught to "press toward the mark." They must discover a faith like Paul's which enabled him to say, "I can do all things through Christ." They must be enabled by being equipped for service. Through providing church leader training, a church can help its members develop in this way.

The discovery of persons with a potential to lead requires understanding of inactive members as well as the ability to direct the activities of the active and interested few. Methods for discovery include a Christian service survey, recommendations from leaders presently serving, observation of people in action, study and analysis of church rolls, and consideration of professional skills which can be adapted for church service.

Recruiting persons to participate in training activities is best accomplished through personal invitations. Recruiting activities range from directing the eager into the right activities to persuading the reluctant to try. Encouraging, urging, praying—all are involved in the recruiting process.

Planning and conducting training opportunities to meet needs is the critical stage of church leader training. Necessary details for getting training underway must be planned and carried out. These include: enlisting leaders to conduct training sessions, assigning suitable space, providing equipment and materials for training, and establishing a system for reporting on training accomplished.

Much church leader training can be provided through short-term training projects designed to meet the needs of the groups involved. In addition to training groups, however, a church should make full use of materials and equipment designed for individualized instruction (self-instruction). Many leaders who cannot be reached for training groups may be willing to study such materials on their own. Programed instruction, individual study guides, workbooks, audio-visual materials and equipment should be provided for this purpose.

A church may also train through providing guided observation and supervised practice in real situations.

Assisting leaders in participating in associational leader training opportunities is another means of providing the training needed.

A church should take advantage of latest methods and materials available to provide a variety of training opportunities and schedules to meet its leader training needs.

When leader training has been established, a church should seek constant improvement of the training opportunities provided. Evaluation should include a careful analysis of the preparations made, organization, schedules, and training procedures. It should also include an appraisal of the trainee as he is training and as he completes leader training experiences. The best evidence of effective church leader training is the readiness of trainees to assume leadership roles.

The scope of the leader training provided by a church will be influenced by:

—the excellence of leadership desired
—the number of trained leaders needed
—the leadership available to conduct the training
—the resources and facilities available for providing the training

In a small church, or a church just beginning leader training, the training may be administered by the Adult department director of church member training. In some churches it may be practical for the director of QUEST to be responsible for leader training and to enlist instructors for leader training courses as they are offered. In other (especially large) churches, leader training may require that a director of church leader training be elected to lead a department for this distinctive ministry. The director of church leader training serves as an associate to the director of QUEST with primary responsibility for training church leaders.

All leader training in a church should be coordinated through the church council. The council may ask the director of QUEST to lead in developing a coordinated leader training plan. The director of church leader training should assist the QUEST director as needed.

To each organization in a church belongs the responsibility for training its own leaders. Any organization may request the director of QUEST to arrange or provide such training. If such requests are not made, the QUEST director may take the initiative to offer leader training opportunities to other church organizations.

2. The Benefits of Church Leader Training

A church may expect to derive certain benefits from each activity or program which makes up its total ministry. What benefits may a church expect from effective church leader training?

By providing church leader training, a church can have an adequate supply of leaders. In fact, a church may build up a reservoir of trained leaders in excess of its present needs.

Effective leader training will produce trained leaders—leaders who are committed and equipped for service to the Lord and to his church. Reclaiming undeveloped church members and redirecting them into useful service can be one of the greatest benefits of church leader training.

Another benefit of leader training is a continuing improvement in leadership performance. Every good leader desires to improve the quality of his service. Effective church leader training will help him fulfil this desire. He may bring to an assignment many other qualifications, but his performance usually depends upon the kind of training he has received. Awareness that his performance is continually improving is often the motivation he needs to continue training.

Steady progress toward the achievement of church goals can be another benefit of church leader training. Rarely does a church exceed the vision, ideals, and plans of its leaders. A church needs leaders who are committed to its goals, and who know how to lead in achieving them. Effective leader training includes a strong emphasis upon the mission of the church. It equips the leader to help move his church to fulfil this mission.

Church leader training also helps develop an increasing number of committed followers. People follow leaders rather than programs. Baptists need strong leaders, but there is also a need for dedicated and committed followers. Developing, inspiring, dedicated leaders will also help at least indirectly in enlisting the followers needed to carry on the work of the church.

QUEST FOR COMMUNICATION

QUEST joins other church programs in fulfilling the task assignment "Provide and interpret information regarding the work of the church and the denomination." This task means informing church members of the work the church does on its own and in cooperation with others. It also includes explaining the meaning of the information provided so that church members may understand it sufficiently to relate appropriately to the work and participate meaningfully in it. An informed church is more likely to be an active and productive church.

If the challenges of the seventies are to be met, it is important for Southern Baptists to work together toward worthy objectives. Coordination and cooperation are possible only when the lines of communication are kept open between church members and denominational leaders. The performance of this task should result in more meaningful participation in the life and work of the church and denomination.

ACCEPTING THE CHALLENGE

A church is incomplete without the benefits which QUEST can provide. The tasks of the training program must be accomplished if a church is to function effectively. QUEST is the church disciplining itself in training. It is the church equipping itself for service.

How can a church expect to be the people of God and to function as the people of God
* if its members know little of Christian doctrine or Christian ethics?
* if its members lack appreciation for its history, its practice, and its procedures?
* if it ignores or neglects the special needs of its new members?
* if its members are not trained to worship, witness, learn, minister, and apply the gospel in daily living?

- if it does not provide training for its leaders, both those already serving and those with leadership potential?

What an important list of tasks! Those who serve their church in the space age through QUEST face a tremendous challenge. It is the challenge to rise above a "business-as-usual" attitude toward training. In every realm about us—in business, in education, in professional circles—training is a must. It is an imperative not only for growth and progress, but for survival itself.

Can churches afford to consider training any less important?

Can untrained church members spread the good news of Christ in an increasingly sophisticated and unreceptive world? Both the Scriptures and reason answer that church members must grow in knowledge, understanding, and skill. What response will the churches make in the seventies? Surely they will answer with a renewed commitment to the imperative of training for the work of Christian service!

9. Church Program and Administrative Services

The seventies will reportedly witness the advent of a society that is increasingly complex and specialized. This society will require consultants and specialists that are trained to provide information and consultation to those in decision-making positions. It will be impossible for the decision makers to stay abreast of the many details, possibilities, and resources that are related to their work. Service institutions that provide this specialized consultation, information, and resources will be necessary in the immediate future.

Churches will also have a need for specialized consultation. They will come to depend increasingly more on consultative and supportive services within their church structure. These services are composed of tasks that assist or serve a church and its programs in order that they may be more efficient and effective. There are two types of church services: program services and administrative services. Each has its unique area of activity in the life of a church.

Church program services provide information, consultation, and resources that assist the church and its programs in their work. The two program services are the library service and the recreation service.

Church administrative services assist a church in its administrative work. The administrative requirements of a church become increasingly heavy and complex as a church grows larger. As a result, a church must turn to committees, the church council, and general church officers for assistance in continuing administrative activities. These services provide the assistance necessary for efficiency in church administration.

PROGRAM SERVICES

Baptist churches in the seventies will face an intensified need for at least two program services: (1) the library service, carried in the church by the library staff, and (2) the recreation service, carried by the recreation staff.

1. Recreation Service

A church, realizing its responsibility for the "whole" man, has the recreation service. Through recreation the church has the opportunity to reach out in its witness and involvement as a powerful Christian force in the community and the world.

(1) *The need for the recreation service.*—Recreation is one avenue to reach the lost. For some persons, it becomes the most important way for contact to be made as the Holy Spirit works, using persons and situations to bring a sinner under conviction. The nature of recreation activities lends itself to meaningful interpersonal relationships. The Christian witnesses in word and deed by showing his true colors in the actual life situations of stress, challenge, temptation, and discipline experienced in recreation activities. Often, contact with the lost will come outside the church building. Recreation makes a natural avenue for outreach to the community. Such opportunities may come through sports leagues, folk musical productions, dramatic presentations, tournaments, and joint use of facilities. For an individual and/or group, an important point of contact is spectator and player participation in school, civic, and public recreation.

Every life needs balance. The Christian's life is no exception. Appropriately chosen recreation, entered into with enthusiasm, can do much to counterbalance the pressures of modern living. It can add spice to the sameness of routine chores. The balanced life must know "re-creation" that brings refreshment and renewal.

In any locale, a church's fellowship knows the disrupting influences stemming from the fast pace of living, rapid transportation, and a generally accepted impersonal approach to life. There are more threats to fellowship for churches with large membership, or churches whose members are forced to drive hundreds of miles each year to attend services. The recreation service of a church has a unique role in helping to build a feeling of togetherness. Recreation activities in a relaxed atmosphere encourage the individual to be himself without having to put up a front. With unfeigned honesty, the church constituency know one another better, understand one another's needs, and find mutual acceptance.

(2) *New ideas for the recreation service.*—Many concepts for the recreation service that have been theoretical are now gaining acceptance. Basic philosophies that get results continue to be the fundamentals of the church recreation service. A prime example is that good leadership and worthy programing are far more important than extensive facilities.

The wide use of recreation techniques and creative programing with recreation establishes recreation in its distinct place as a church program service. The church has an obligation to itself and the community to have good recreation facilities, staffed by qualified leaders and accessible to all. In a few instances this could mean building a recreation facility. More important is the church's willingness to go beyond its walls to provide recreation (for example, softball teams in the community of the mission church). In this way, recreation has the potential of becoming a point of contact for enlistment, evangelism, or Bible study. Recreation can also have a meaningful role as it helps to meet the needs of special groups such as internationals, aging, mentally retarded, delinquents, and alcoholics.

There is a growing awareness among Christians that they are the church in the business world, civic meetings, and the academic setting. Perhaps this should be felt even more strongly by the Christian in the recreation setting. The challenge is great because of the multiple and scattered recreation opportunities. Many Christians own beach homes, mountain retreats, farms and houseboats that become second homes. The four-day work week often makes for active participation in dual churches. When there is not a church at the resort site, the opportunities for sharing one's faith may take the form of campfire services, vespers, story hours, mountain sunrise devotionals, play readings, nature hikes, or gospel songfests.

A church's recreation service should carefully analyze its activities and become broad enough to include all worthwhile recreation interests. It continues to endorse only those activities that provide socially accepted self-expression of body and mind. Along with this should go the choosing of the activity for the purpose of giving joy and fun with no regrets to the individual and/or the group.

Many of today's senior adults are capable of leading recreation for others as well as their own group. This untapped source of recreation leadership has limitless possibilities.

Many people discover the out-of-doors through recreation. The recreation service assists the church in programed outdoor religious education. The recreation service is also responsible for seeing that there is training in appreciation of, and skills for, outdoor recreation.

(3) *New structures for the recreation service.*—The purposes of church recreation are: to develop Christian personality, to win persons to Christ, and to aid the total church program in every way possible. To accomplish these purposes the recreation service has two tasks.

a. *Provide recreation.*—In providing recreation the recreation service gives general guidance and assistance in fellowship and recreation activities. The recreation service is responsible for providing opportunities for the church constituency to have wholesome, creative leisure-time experiences. In some of these the recreation service has full initiative. It programs recreation as a service to the church (for example, softball teams, basketball teams, family camping, all-church picnic) .

The recreation service complements, undergirds, and strengthens the Bible teaching program by becoming a workshop in everyday Christian living. All program leaders may look to the recreation service for assistance in the use of recreation techniques.

In providing opportunities for informal singing at fellowships, parties, banquets, and retreats, the recreation service may take the initiative. It calls on the music program as needed.

Some mission action takes the form of recreation activity, and other mission action includes recreation. In either case, the missions program takes the initiative.

Pastoral ministries may call on the recreation service to provide drama or other recreation to assist in proclaiming the gospel. In providing recreation, the recreation service assists pastoral ministries in caring for the church members and other persons in the community.

The training program will look to the recreation service to provide recreation that will enhance new member orientation, member training, and leader training. The training program, calling on the recreation service as needed, will provide church members with opportunities for:

(1) training in making wholesome recreation a vital part of their Christian lives

(2) training in the skills of using leisure time as a means of increasing their own general personal effectiveness in worshiping, witnessing, learning, ministering, and applying the Christian faith in life.

b. *Provide consultation, leadership assistance, and resources in recreation.*—The recreation service more often operates in carrying out this second task than the first. The recreation service takes the initiative in informing all leaders of available helps in recreation and encouraging their use.

It will be through the cooperative efforts with the church council that the recreation service will correlate its consultation and other leadership assistance. The recreation service is dependent on the congregation for providing resources—physical, financial, and human.

As a resource center for the church, the library service makes available to recreation leaders printed and audiovisual resources.

(4) *New adventures open to recreation.*—Church recreation faces new and exciting opportunities in the seventies as new vistas open to the service.

All trends point to more leisure time in the future for the average man as the thirty-hour week becomes a reality. Because of the impact and the effects of the new leisure, some observers call it a leisure revolution. Creative programing, using recreation, can do much to head off problems resulting from individuals unprepared for leisure use. Among these are the worker who earns an increasing salary for a decreasing number of hours; the unemployed; the young; and the individual reaching retirement.

Unbound by four walls and true to the example of the New Testament church, today's church considers its responsibility. Without apology it should become identified with the community. Youth and young adults can go into shopping centers and outdoor theaters singing folk music that conveys the gospel message. In mission action the church can use recreation to reach the inner city with the good news.

The church in seeking to meet family needs can appropriately turn to the recreation service. Some needs will be met through family recreation programed at the church, as well as skill training for, and encouragement in, family recreation at home. Home recreation includes sports, games, and creative activities chosen according to the family tastes and interests. The growth in family camping provides the opportunity for every church to build fellowship around the campfire. The unforgettable experience of meditating on spiritual truths while watching the dying embers of an open fire may now be shared by adults as well as young people. These and other expanding horizons for recreation will bring new opportunities for Christianity to show its relevancy to the day and the hour.

In an affluent society more recreation activities are available to more people. Today every third family owns a boat. Vacationers travel at various times of the year to places near and far.

The recreation service should major on creativity in activities and techniques. One innovation is the recreation revival. This uses drama, fellowships, parties, dinners, and retreats to involve both saved and unsaved. Portable stages and other recreation equipment will aid in taking recreation to where the people are. For the aging, creativity will help to assure that old age brings new enjoyments.

2. Library Service

What has been said of education in the public schools is equally true in the church: "A liberal education may begin in the schoolroom, but it will not rise above mediocrity unless it is extended into the library. Without library influences, we go stoop-shouldered and limping through life. Without library influences, we resemble flimsy stuff that does not wear well." [1] For a dynamic church to offer a quality educational program, it may be said that the library service is indispensable to the seventies; should be in step with the seventies; can be structured for the seventies; and must be involved in the adventure of the seventies.

(1) *Indispensable to the seventies.*—"Go ye therefore, and teach." Whatever else Jesus had in mind for his church, he intended that it teach. In support of this command, W. L. Howse has said: "A teaching church needs a library as much as [does] a college, university, or seminary." Because this is true, the library service is vitally involved in the educational program of today's churches. This involvement will steadily increase during the seventies.

Baptist churches are in the business of educating. Buildings, organizations, and programs are planned for that purpose. We do not, however, provide Christian education in a vacuum. The church is only one of many institutions involved in education. Schools enhance learning by television and other modern teaching media. New teaching methods, rapid advances in teaching-learning media, and the ever enlarging store of accumulated knowledge require churches to provide resources that will help keep Christian education in step with our times.

It has been estimated: "Man has accumulated more knowledge since World War II than he had accumulated since the beginning of time. The speed of this accumulation seems to be racing ever faster." [2] Our churches now face the overwhelming task of finding ways to provide that part of this knowledge needed in Christ's work. Baptists cannot hope to "digest" into periodicals all the information required. We can, however, provide a core curriculum through dated media. This core can then be backed up with a stockpile of library resources.

The library service is also indispensable as a means of getting

---

[1] John Snider, *I Love Books* (Washington: Review Herald Publishing Association, 1944) , p. 75.

[2] Ernest J. Loessner, *Adults Continuing to Learn* (Nashville: Convention Press, 1967) , p. 35.

to people where they are and when they are interested. It is increasingly difficult to "gather a crowd" for periods of time necessary for good teaching-learning situations. If, therefore, a church is to reach and teach, it must find ways of getting to people at their convenience. We must make the gospel message available when the man on the move pauses long enough to open his mind and his heart. Frequently, this pause is at a point of crisis. Here, again, resources can meet needs even when the presence of a teacher is impossible.

"For the future, the library service is essential to the success of the training program in the church." And what Philip B. Harris has said about the library service and the training program is true of every phase of church life. No longer can the development and use of the library service be optional. To meet the challenge of the seventies, the library service is indispensable.

(2) *In step with the seventies.*—A "service" is defined as a contribution to the welfare of others. A library service is an activity related to printed or audiovisual media which provides enrichment or assistance to individuals or programs. Baptist churches seeking to meet the challenge of the seventies will face a need for an expanded concept of the library service. As a concept of work, the library service speaks to a plan which assigns to the library staff all the library-type activities of a church. To be in step with the seventies this service should be collecting, conserving, and circulating all types of educational media (books, audiovisuals, et cetera) ; printed materials education; and, at the option of the music program, the music library operation.

The combination of print and nonprint teaching materials into a single resource center is in tune with the most advance trends in public education. When a single organization can specialize in providing and guiding in the use of communication media, the entire educational program is strengthened. It is for this reason that school libraries are becoming "Instructional Media Programs." This is also the reason for huge government grants aimed at increasing the quality of media services in all levels of public education.

The church of the seventies cannot afford to be less interested in media than public educators. The library service offers to the church the opportunity to make its educational methodology and subject content consistent in quality with its building expenditures. The library service also offers the over and beyond content for the person whose intellectual and interest needs take him beyond the pages of lesson course materials. People in the seventies will be searching for answers. Through an adequate library service the church gives them a place to look.

(3) *Structured for the seventies.*—The library service will be structured for the seventies around these tasks:

- Provide printed and audiovisual resources
- Promote printed and audiovisual resources
- Consult with church leaders and members in the use of printed and audiovisual resources

a. To provide printed and audiovisual resources is to make available to the church (programs and individuals) the printed and audiovisual media needed to do its work. Providing resources involves at least four distinct activities: selecting, processing, circulating, and maintaining.

The challenge of providing resources can be caught only as it is translated into life situations. For example, a pastor shared with a library worker his burden for an unsaved doctor. Repeated attempts to help the man see his need for Christ were met with "intellectual" excuses. God could not be analyzed, the doctor reasoned; therefore, he did not exist.

It was suggested that the pastor share with the unsaved doctor a copy of *The Evidence of God in an Expanding Universe* by John Clover Monsma. This book is a collection of testimonies of faith by a group of forty scientists. Each of these men is a recognized authority in his given field.

In a few weeks, the pastor came again to the library worker and said: "The book did not do it, but the Holy Spirit used the book to help bring conviction. Last Sunday morning the doctor made a public profession of faith."

Providing resources offers equal rewards as the church reaches out beyond the walls of its building. For example, the high-rise apartments of large cities have provided for many persons an impenetrable fortress. Here persons can withdraw in privacy from all intrusions—even the influence of the gospel.

In one city, a certain minister's interest in people intensified into concern for these modern cliff dwellers. If an outsider could not reach them, he and his family would become insiders, he decided. By leasing an apartment, he made himself and his services as a minister in residence available to all his neighbors. A second apartment was rented for use as a reading, counseling, and prayer area. Library resources were provided to be used in interest-related cultivation and to extend the Bible teaching efforts of the minister's family.

b. To promote the use of printed and audiovisual resources means to make known the presence and purpose of library resources. It may also be called advertising or publicity. In an age when persons are bombarded with thousands of ideas daily, competition for attention is high. Library resources and services must be kept constantly before the people in an appealing way.

Promotion is an effort to create an awareness of a need. Many educators consider it a form of guidance. Lucile F. Fargo has said in *The Library in the School*: "To stimulate the desire to use printed materials therefore becomes a most important function of the library. . . . American boys and girls read, but they do not read the right things. Surrounded by reading materials, the majority of which are mediocre or sensational, they face the ever-present temptations to read the 'worse' rather than the 'better' publications. . . . To increase reading of the better publications to the proportional decrease of the worse, the reader must be led to prefer them by sympathetic and, usually, individual guidance." [3]

What has been said about promotion of printed media applies to the promotion of audiovisual media as well. Indeed, the promotion task of the library service suggests that good promotional techniques will be used to create an awareness of all types of educational media, an understanding of their teaching capabilities, and a desire to use them for personal growth and program assignment.

For the seventies, this task demands the best in skills and commitment.

c. To consult with church leaders and members in the value and use of printed and audiovisual resources is to inform individuals and groups in the value and skills of using library resources.

It is in the area of consultation that the library service will find

---

[3] Chicago: American Library Association, 1947, pp. 35, 39.

its greatest challenge. This is an age of electronic communication. Now as never before churches need persons who are willing to become media specialists—persons who know what is available and how it can be used to communicate spiritual truths.

This is illustrated in a situation where a minister became involved, almost accidentally, in the lives of three youths in their first brush with the law. He happened to be in a store when the boys were brought in to be identified in connection with a theft. The minister was able to get the boys' names and addresses. Before following up with a visit in their homes, he sought help from a library staff member. What was available that might be used to establish rapport and to make an impression on these first offenders?

The library worker suggested the use of the recorded testimonies of five state prison inmates: "This tape speaks directly to the boys' situation." Then, the library staff member added: "But, before you go, would you like me to run through the tape with you?"

The minister answered: "That would be most helpful. I could use a little help on operating the recorder, too."

Immediately the minister became the learner, and the library worker became the consultant. The consultation was informal, and it was with a single individual. Most of all, it was effective. The tape was edited. Two of the five testimonies were chosen. They agreed on two possible plans for using the tape—one for the family, and one for the boys. No less important was the practice gained by the minister in using the equipment effectively.

Not all consultation need be individual, however. If church leaders are to make the most effective use of educational media, the church must offer a continuous program of educating in how, when, and which media to use to accomplish desired ends. No leader-training program is complete until participants have been given orientation and instruction in using the total resources of the library.

The potential of modern media to spread the gospel and to make learning effective is limited only by the church's willingness to elect persons to the library staff and to train them to guide in the use of all media.

(4) *Involved in the adventure of the seventies.*—The

library staff that responds to the challenge of the seventies will
magnify the many new communication media. And the church
which utilizes them will strengthen its teaching, training, witnessing, and ministering efforts.

There are many exciting uses of library resources which involve relating to a person at a point of interest or need. Though
largely untapped, this opportunity is not unexplored. Many
churches are using library resources in fulfilling the functions
of worshiping, proclaiming, education, and ministering.

a. *Worship.*—Consider, for instance, the group who used
slides and recordings in a series of devotionals at a church retreat.
A theme was chosen for each morning's devotions. Scripture
passages and songs were chosen to match the theme. Each day
the group sang one hymn, and the Scripture passage was read.
A recording was played while slides illustrating the message
of the song were projected. This was followed by a period of
meditation and prayer.

In addition to this use of resources to aid in worship, churches
also may use such media to take worship beyond the walls of
the building. Many churches are in a position to consider recording worship services on video tape. These taped services can
then be taken to home-bound persons. (Video tape also supplies
an audio and visual record of outstanding events in the life of
the church.)

b. *Proclaim.*—The reading room is an avenue of proclamation which holds great potential for Baptists. Many churches and
associations have seen the value of such an approach and have
begun to use it. In shopping centers, downtown areas, and
trailer parks, reading rooms already have established spearheads
for witnessing.

Film revivals also have proved an effective means of proclaiming the gospel. This is a revival effort in which selected films
are used as the "sermon." The song service and invitation are
used much in the same way as in a "preaching" revival service.
Experience with this approach to revival has seen decisions in
all areas of Christian concern brought about by the Holy Spirit's
use of the filmed witness.

c. *Educate.*—Much of what has been said in earlier parts of this section deals with the place of media in Christian education. Some examples of what this means in actual practice may be helpful here.

There is, for instance, the Sunday School department director who makes reading assignments to teachers prior to planning teachers meetings. This leader recognizes the need for information which goes beyond the scope of lesson course materials.

In another church a study leader of an Adult training class spends several hours each week gathering from library resources information to be assigned to members of the study group. The result has been Adults actively involved in finding answers to many of life's vital questions.

Still another approach to education with library resources is what one pastor calls the "Pastor's Parchment Club." This pastor gets a commitment from persons to read specific books. He then meets with these persons as a group and leads in a time of dialogue. Open discussion on the subject of the book helps all persons gain insight into many pertinent subjects.

d. *Minister.*—The use of library resources in ministering to persons in need finds many avenues of expression. There is, for instance, the example set by a church in the Appalachians. Much has been written and filmed to document the needs of families in this area. Not so well known is what is being done by Christians who live there. Concern for the children in the many cabin homes in the mountains around their town motivated a certain church to take action. One of the first ministries was a mobile library. A secondhand mail truck was equipped with shelves and stocked with books. These materials have been the means which have opened many opportunities to witness to the saving power of Christ and to express Christian concern over needs discovered.

Another use of library resources in ministering is represented by a pastor who uses them in his counseling ministry. Each person with whom he counsels is sent to the library with a prescription for a book which speaks to his area of need.

Still another means of ministering is illustrated by a church which makes library materials a regular part of its hospital ministry. One such incident resulted in a salvation experience by the patient. During the course of the first visit by a church member, the patient expressed her interest in flowers. The alert visitor took this as a point of contact. On the next visit he brought *Voiceless Lips* by Nell Outlaw. The interest shown by the visitor and the witness of this book were used by the Holy Spirit to bring the unsaved patient to a personal acceptance of Christ as Saviour.

Each of these examples represents a church which has already become involved in the adventure of using media in fulfilling its functions. But many of the most exciting adventures are ahead as churches look to the library service in their churches for assistance in providing

- Bibliotherapy
- Personal reading and study instructions
- Cassette and cartridge tapes and recorders
- Rapid reading machines
- Microfilming
- Video tape equipment
- Career corners
- Programed learning equipment and materials
- Study carrels
- Realia (curios, objects, and so forth)
- Audiovisual viewing tables
- Listening centers
- Music materials and equipment
- Field-trip information
- Drama materials and props
- Instruction in the use of audiovisuals

There are in each of the tasks assigned to the library service challenges that demand the best from those who serve. Because of this demand, the most capable Christians should be sought for the library staff. They should be dedicated and practicing Christians, marked by a radiating desire to serve. They deserve maximum support from the church. The library service should have the most desirable location and an adequate budget. The school principal of Granby, Massachusetts, expressed the philosophy which should prevail: "The librarian is so vital to the improvement of instruction that it would be foolhardy not to supply maximum support."

ADMINISTRATIVE SERVICES

Church administrative services are those activities performed by church officers, the church council, and committees to assist a church in the implementation of its administrative tasks. Churches need the assistance of individuals and groups to carry out their administrative work. The church assembled cannot hope to care for every administrative need it faces. A church can work better if it can limit its work to decision-making and allow others to study, plan, and recommend administrative procedures and solutions to administrative problems. Church officers, the church council, and committees provide this assistance.

1. Church Administrative Tasks

Every Baptist church has certain administrative tasks that must be performed regularly by its members to move it forward in its work for Christ. These tasks provide guidance for the work of the church and relate to decisions that can be made only by the gathered church—decisions that cannot be delegated to lesser church groups. The church administrative tasks are:

- Govern the life and work of the church under the lordship of Christ.
- Determine the church's programs, program services, and administrative services.
- Establish organization to conduct and/or coordinate the church's programs and services.
- Determine the church's cooperative work with other churches.
- Establish and maintain appropriate external relationships.
- Select pastor, staff, and volunteer leaders and assign responsibilities.
- Provide and allocate resources for the total work of the church.

Work related to these tasks is assigned by the church to church officers, the church council, and committees. Although church officers are administrative servants of the church, they perform tasks that are unlike those normally assigned to the church council and committees. Church officers assist the church in continuing administrative activities while the church council and committee activities may properly be referred to as study and planning tasks or administrative services tasks.

2. Administrative Services Tasks

Those tasks assigned to the church council and committees are primarily study and planning tasks although continuing administrative work may be assigned by the church at any time. The church must make its administrative decisions, but it wisely does so on the basis of study and planning done by its service groups.

On the following pages attention is given to the content area of each administrative services task, an appraisal of trends in the area at present, and a statement of some of the central issues facing the churches in each area during the 1970's.

(1) *Conduct studies and prepare plans for governing the life and work of the church under the lordship of Christ; administer approved plans as assigned.*—A Baptist church is a self-governing body. It is independent of outside control and responsible to God for its life and work.

Each Baptist church must develop its own constitution, bylaws, articles of faith, and convenant. These documents state the rules regulating the church's life.

Often in the course of Baptist history, churches have alternately emphasized or deemphasized their right to self-determination. Most recently the churches have stressed cooperation. As a result, denominational ties have been strong and some church independence has given way to custom and cooperative action.

During the sixties, signs of a renewed emphasis on local church autonomy became increasingly evident. The characteristics of transition and change evident in the world at large are also being detected in the churches. More and more churches seem to be showing a preference for self-determination in every area of their lives. Self-understanding and self-renewal movements are placing the church at the center of interest among its people.

In the seventies, churches will of necessity make governmental decisions about their internal structure, theology, denominational ties, membership practices, and direction. Serious study and planning by church groups about areas hitherto taken for granted may become a common occurrence. Very little in the life of a church will escape the questioning and exploring spirit of the age. Church government may undergo a transformation because of an increasing desire of the laity to be heard on all church issues. The churches may see during the seventies the sternest test in history of their ideals about congregational government.

Administrative services should be used fully in areas of church government in the future. Churches will need to depend more and more on smaller groups within their membership to study, plan, and be informed about issues and procedures. Churches will be turning to these groups for direction and assistance in solving the complex problems they face.

(2) *Conduct studies and prepare plans for the church's future course; administer approved plans as assigned.*—Seldom in recent history has there been more uncertainly about the direction churches will take in the future. The confidence that has been an outstanding characteristic of churches since the days of the Great Depression is being replaced by a spirit of seeking uncertainty. Forces at work in the sixties have stirred the churches to reexamine their mission, purpose, and objectives.

The quest for meaning will continue with even more momentum during the seventies. Churches will struggle to define and express their God-given mission to humanity. A debate about evangelism and ethics may grow to the proportions of the social gospel issue at the beginning of the century.

Church planning should become a more meaningful administrative tool during the seventies. Annual and long-range planning will be needed by the churches to define and carry out their mission. As the churches depend more on themselves for direction and meaning, they will be forced to plan their work. Denominational assistance will become more flexible in the seventies, and churches will be forced to make decisions about alternate approaches to their work. This freedom will be attended by a new responsibility in study and planning by the churches. The gathered church will be turning to groups within its membership for assistance in defining purpose and direction.

(3) *Conduct studies and prepare plans for establishing and coordinating the church's programs and services; administer approved plans as assigned.*—Many churches discovered the principles and techniques of programing during the sixties. With the concept came new visions of church work. The church could be seen as a single, coordinate organizational entity with purpose

and direction for its structure and action. Church activity could be need oriented and designed individually by each church to meet the unique needs of its community.

The strength of the programing concept is the emphasis it places on the church. Each church must develop the program it needs. This strength also became a hindrance during the sixties because the creative energies it called for from church and denominational personnel were not always available and willing to be given.

Programing in the seventies will be even more needful. Churches will be rethinking their structure and work. They will be deciding what work they will do and how to do it. Evaluation, planning, and coordination of church work will be increasingly necessary. The creative work of the church council and committees to plan and coordinate will no longer be a luxury.

Already some churches are rethinking their approaches and structures. There is a mood for change that seems to be increasingly pervasive. Traditional approaches to education and outreach are being redesigned. This trend to change will continue through the seventies as new educational approaches are introduced in public education, and as innovations in communications media open new outreach techniques for churches.

Increasing opportunities and approaches will require a creative response from the church council and committees.

(4) *Conduct studies and prepare plans for establishing and maintaining the church's relationship; administer approved plans as assigned.*—The ties a church makes between itself and other Christian, sectarian, and nonsectarian groups should be the result of deliberate thought and decision. Reasons for, and result of, these relationships should be carefully weighed by a church.

Existing patterns of relationships among Baptist churches have developed deliberately through Baptist history. The associations, state conventions, and the Southern Baptist Convention and its agencies are products of the struggle of the churches to develop sound means for cooperative work that reflect biblical principles and congregational church polity.

Relationships will not escape the testing spirit that appears certain to be manifest in the seventies. Already, some state conventions and associations are in the throes of relationship struggles that have been brought about by unusual doctrinal practices among their churches.

Relationships among the churches of other faiths and the state will continue to be an issue. The necessity for each church to continuously consider its situation and make its decisions about its relationships will not lessen.

The church will continue to bear the burden for decisions made in this area of its life. Study and planning will be increasingly necessary to define, establish, and maintain those relationships into which a church enters.

(5) *Conduct studies and prepare plans for allocating the church's leadership, facilities, and financial resources; administer approved plans as assigned.*—The increasing affluence of the churches will require serious soul-searching about the proper disposition of church resources during the seventies. Traditional approaches to the use of resources will need refinement and in some cases redefinition.

Baptist churches have become increasingly wealthy in talent and material possessions since World War II. With this wealth has come the responsibility for its wise use in the work of the kingdom of God. Churches are controlling millions of dollars and have at their beck and call the time and talents of some of the country's most able citizens. The potential of this vast wealth is immeasurable.

Skepticism about the investments of churches is already showing itself. The most basic seems to concern the percentage of resources being used on buildings and furnishings over against that used in witness and ministry outside the walls of the churches. Some feel that soon the churches will have to give serious consideration to whether their material possessions help or hinder their work among people.

The seventies will not see the churches finding easy solutions to these resource problems. They will see the churches seriously struggling to find ways to best use their resources to help persons find Jesus Christ.

The volume of change facing the churches in the seventies will require them to make many major decisions. These decisions should not be made without careful study and planning.

As the decade progresses, the role of church administrative services will become increasingly significant in the life of the church.

Therefore, churches should seek to renew the structure and approaches of their administrative services. They should be concerned that capable and spiritually sensitive persons are elected to carry out these responsibilities.

Conclusion

"Not by might, nor by power, but by my spirit, saith the Lord of hosts" (Zech. 4:6).

The people of God today must not forget this proclamation made centuries ago to Zerubbabel and the people of the Promised Land. God declared a fact that must control his people throughout the ages. Men will never accomplish God's purpose at any time in history through might or power structures they establish.

Today men, sometimes Christian men, are determined to bring about God's will on earth through the use of their personal power. Today is a period of standoffs and showdowns between men who control things the way they are and men who want to use force to change things. Our world is going to be different because of these conflicts. Schisms and turmoil already are clearly visible throughout the communities of our nation. Can might and power used by men who have a spirit of rule or ruin ever establish a world in which the will of God prevails? The answer obviously is no! How then can churches have hope? How can we face the seventies without fear? When the disciples were being tossed about on the stormy Sea of Galilee, as men are in today's world, they anxiously and fearfully called to the Lord for help. He responded in action by calming the sea. He responded in word by saying, "Why are ye so fearful? how is it that ye have no faith?" (Mark 4:40).

Faith which lives by the spirit of God is essential in the organized structure of a church if God's purpose is to be accomplished. It is a faith which is found and expressed in our prayers to God. The people of God and their organizational structures may be as up-to-date as an American spaceship. However, without the indwelling of the Holy Spirit, they will be as useless as a fuelless spaceship on the launching pad at Cape Kennedy.

In addition to developing new organization structures, churches must *wait* for God to add his Spirit. When the disciples waited in the upper room at Jerusalem, they had already been given their mission (Matthew 28:18–20). They had already been told by whose might and power they would act. But still the Lord insisted that they wait for this power to become personal. He "commanded them that they should not depart from Jerusalem, but wait for the promise of the Father. . . . Ye shall receive power, after that the Holy Ghost is come upon you" (Acts 1:4,8).

Can we believe that having prepared our churches structurally for mission we must discipline ourselves to wait for God's Spirit? Such waiting may require of God's people a greater faith than is required for doing most of what churches are doing now. Prayerful waiting is a forgotten or depreciated experience in the busy activity of many modern churches and Christians. This was not so with our Lord who said: " 'Have faith in God! I solemnly say to you, whoever says to this mountain, "Get up and throw yourself into the sea," and does not doubt at all in his heart, but has faith that what he says will take place, shall have it. So then I tell you, whenever you pray and ask for anything, have faith that it has been granted you, and you will get it' " (Mark 11:22–24, Williams).

There are mountains of problems in the world of the seventies. Men, women, and children are universally weighed down under their own mountains of hopelessness. Who will go to the rescue? Who will cast their mountains into the sea? Can a church be so filled by the Spirit of God that it will push out into our mad world without regard for itself? No structure of the seventies can succeed that lacks a spirit of openness and freedom to act without first counting the personal cost. This was Christ's spirit. " 'If anyone wants to be my disciple, he must say, "No" to self, put the cross on his shoulders, and keep on following me. For whoever wants to save his higher life, will have to give up the lower life, and whoever gives up his lower life for me and for the good news, will save the higher life' " (Mark 8:34–35, Williams).

Jesus Christ came down from heavenly places into a world of sin, into a world where every man was a slave to evil. He came not in a spirit of fear or hate or pride. He came as a servant. His spirit led him to every corner of his small nation, to all parts of the cities and open country, and to persons with every kind of human problem. His spirit caused him to weep, to console, to heal, to challenge, to feed, and to forgive. Whatever men needed to overcome evil or its results, he loved them enough to give. The Lord's spirit of love caused him to go because people lacked faith to come. The spirit of churches in the seventies must be like our Lord. We must be structured organizationally to go into the world. We must go not as the pride of our community but as the servants of all people. We must find the back streets and back countries of our communities and world. We must locate people where they are having their problems. We must weep with them, laugh with them, console them, challenge them, feed them, and forgive them. We must go because in the seventies so few will have faith to come. We must go because men need the good news of God's love in order to overcome evil and its results.

Spirit *and* structure are necessary if a church is going to be dynamic. In faith those who fear well-established and effectively organized church structure must lay this fear aside. In faith those who fear a spirit that causes churches to feel emotional concern for people must lay this fear aside. In the seventies, a church will have magnificent opportunities to use its programs to love people in the name of Christ.

" 'You have heard that it was said, "Love your friends, hate your enemies." But now I tell you: love your enemies, and pray for those who mistreat you, so that you will become the sons of your Father in heaven. For he makes his sun to shine on bad and good people alike, and gives rain to those who do right and those who do wrong. Why should you expect God to reward you, if you love only the people who love you? Even the tax collectors do that! And if you speak only to your friends, have you done anything out of the ordinary? Even the pagans do that! You must be perfect—just as your Father in heaven is perfect' " (Matt. 5: 43–48, TEV).

PERSONAL LEARNING ACTIVITIES

Chapter 1

1. Define "theodemocracy."
2. Give five characteristics of a New Testament church.
3. Define the five functions of a church.

Chapter 2

1. Which parts of life change continuously and which do not?
2. What was Jesus' attitude toward tradition as a basis for faith and practice?
3. What does it mean for a church to be relevant?
4. Why were the churches at Jerusalem and Antioch different?

Chapter 3

1. List three challenges the church must face during the seventies.
2. Who should determine the objective of a church?
3. Define church "task," church "program," and church "service."
4. What is synergism?

Chapter 4

1. Define pastoral ministries.
2. List the pastoral ministries tasks of a church.
3. What church officers normally accomplish pastoral ministries tasks?
4. List four areas of concern that confront pastoral ministries during the seventies.

Chapter 5

1. List the various Bible study approaches that may be used by a church's Bible teaching program to teach the Bible.
2. State the tasks of a church's Bible teaching program.

Chapter 6

1. Define "missions" and "representative missions."
2. What does it mean to teach missions in a church?

3. List the essential actions necessary to teach missions in a church.
4. What does it mean to engage in mission action in a church?
5. List some opportunities a church has for supporting world missions through prayer and giving.

Chapter 7

1. What contemporary forms of music are influencing church music today?
2. Define music "performance" in a church.
3. Define three church music tasks.

Chapter 8

1. What is the new name of the Southern Baptist church training program?
2. List three ways a church training program supports other church programs and services.
3. What are the three types of training offered in the new church training program?
4. List the church training tasks.

Chapter 9

1. Define a church program service.
2. List the library service tasks.
3. List the recreation service tasks.
4. List the administrative services tasks.

Pre-school
children
Youth division
Adult